# Leading Sch

*Leading Schools Through Trauma* is a data-driven resource for education leaders and administrators preparing to help students heal from acute traumas. Traumatizing experiences are inevitable and cyclical, and we see them at individual, local and large-scale levels. As a school leader you need concrete tools to help learners flourish in their wake, especially amid the challenges of our current moment. This book offers a strategic approach to sustaining community wellness and stability, using real-time, short-term data sets accessible to teachers, and guiding students toward incremental, progressive goal-setting. Evidence-based practices for recognizing traumas, scaling formative assessments and providing teachers with problem-based professional development will help you and your staff develop growth plans that are collaborative with and individualized for students.

**Michael S. Gaskell** is Principal of Hammarskjold Middle School in East Brunswick, New Jersey, USA.

# Leading Schools Through Trauma

A Data-Driven Approach to Helping Children Heal

Michael S. Gaskell

Routledge
Taylor & Francis Group

NEW YORK AND LONDON

First published 2022
by Routledge
605 Third Avenue, New York, NY 10158

and by Routledge
2 Park Square, Milton Park, Abingdon, Oxon, OX14 4RN

*Routledge is an imprint of the Taylor & Francis Group, an informa business*

*Library of Congress Cataloging-in-Publication Data*
A catalog record for this book has been requested

ISBN: 978-0-367-75102-9 (hbk)
ISBN: 978-0-367-75562-1 (pbk)
ISBN: 978-1-003-16297-1 (ebk)

DOI: 10.4324/9781003162971

Typeset in Palatino
by Apex CoVantage, LLC

I wish to dedicate this book to my wife, Michele, who has been a guiding light in my life for nearly three decades. She has seen the best version of me and the very worst. Yet she had the audacity to see the promise that lies beyond my worst days and that is a large part of the reason I was committed to writing this book. Hope and courage are the posits that guide us to success and teach our children the way around their challenges.

Thank you, Michele, for helping me model the way.

# Contents

# Meet the Author

Michael S. Gaskell is Principal of Hammarskjold Middle School in East Brunswick, New Jersey, USA, and was formerly a special educator and assistant principal in Paramus, NJ. He continues to model the pursuit of lifelong learning as a mentor to new principals through the New Jersey Leaders to Leaders program and regularly presents on topics relevant to today's educators. The author of *Microstrategy Magic: Confronting Classroom Challenges While Saving Time and Energy* (Rowman & Littlefield, 2020), Dr. Gaskell has published over 20 articles in eSchoolNews, Middleweb, NASSP Smartbrief on EdTech, Education Post and Education Dive, and has made the most-read section of ASCD Smartbrief on multiple occasions.

# Preface

There were numerous reasons for my decision to commit to a text that would aid educators in their day-to-day practice with kids suffering the damaging effects of trauma. First and foremost, this has been very personal for me. Unlike most educators and especially educational leaders, I was not a cookie cutter, Boy Scout, rule following, highly performing student in my own right. In fact, throughout most of my educational years, the prognosis was clear: I was not college-bound nor well-adjusted enough to have a successful adult life. Much of this prognosis was highlighted in a school psychological evaluation as far back as third grade. This is where professionals first began to call me anxious, low performing, hostile and other terms that pointed to the characteristics of trauma.

As I often share with children suffering academic challenges that may or may not be beyond their capacity, I failed math not once but two times in high school. Both times, I had to go to summer school to move forward in my academic career. I had long forgotten and never truly understood the scope of challenges others had observed in me, or my lackluster performance that granted them this perspective. Not until one day just a few years ago, when my young daughter was snooping around my parents' home and found a folder in which it was simply labeled, "Mike."

In that folder contained everything from my third-grade, ill-fated predictions through progress reports that would discourage the most hopeful and those summer school records showing how I barely made it onto the next grade. I am not sure why my parents held onto these records years beyond or how they would have seen them as useful. Yet, I am eternally grateful that they did. They gave me an objective long view of a child that should have and certainly could have had a fate that would have been predictably negative given the characterizations described around my struggles and behavioral challenges.

Decades after this prognosis, I was presenting my dissertation for an educational doctorate. Upon completion of this dissertation, I was asked to wait for a few minutes while my dissertation chair discussed whether I was qualified to be granted a doctoral degree with the committee evaluating me. In those unnerving moments, I thought about how she did not know about the kid who had barely gotten out of high school, or any of the other associated factors that stood in his way. All she knew was I had gotten to this point in an educational leadership doctoral program. She returned from the committee discussion with a sign that read, "Congratulations, Dr. Gaskell!"

The details between these contrasts are a story in their own right. What is important to highlight for the purpose of this text is that much of what allowed me to persevere beyond expected doom was frankly some accidental fortune. The problem with accidental fortune is that most kids do not get those same conditions to set up opportunities for reversals of a dim outlook. Whether those were internal or external factors; in fact, more likely both, we need to provide the structures for kids who have similar obstacles in their way, and that is where this book comes in.

Through research, personal experience and anecdotally time-tested practices, this book lays out these structures in a realistic manner, that allows any busy educator to seize on existing opportunities to help children move beyond the effects of their traumatic circumstances. When I was somehow able to steadily progress in my later early adult life, I saw how factors like resilience propelled me past those early fateful predictions.

When I became a special education teacher early in my career, I learned to apply many of those personal lessons of overcoming predispositions to my young learners who faced a similar fate.

Some of their stories are remarkable successes, others are not. I learned then, that I could not save every child, and to not be disenfranchised that I could not. That was a distraction from the larger goal: if I could move many of these children, much of time, it was better than before. I had to believe this was progress. I became heavily involved in staff development, which sparked my interest in applying research, balanced with the anecdotal experiences of others and myself.

As I dove into research for this text, I wanted to be certain the principles behind it were practical and oriented to those who work so hard every day, in the trenches, with our most at-risk learners. Finding ways to inspire and present options for these professionals was half the battle. I do not just write from my experiences. I back it with research. And I do not just suggest theoretical research. I back it with the practical experiences gained in real places. Places where children show increasing signs that their trauma has injured them, to which we can apply a well-placed Band-Aid that they will someday take off, on their own. They will see and feel the same healing I did decades ago, that sets the stage for remarkable potential and opportunities. That is the single reward I get from sharing this guide with you.

# 1

# Introduction – Our New World Order and How to Help Traumatized Students

Children are showing increased impacts of trauma and the evidence for why is becoming clearer: they suffer from an increased breakdown in the social structures that equip them with the tools to lead a well-balanced life. Werner and Smith (2001) conducted a remarkable, 40-year study on hundreds of individuals from childhood to middle age, demonstrating how they responded to trauma throughout their life. This study revealed incredible and convincing results, which led to important strategies to support the development of individuals and, more importantly, their recovery from trauma.

Werner tracked the developmental stages of these nearly 700 individuals from 1955 until they entered middle age, on the island of Kauai, in Hawaii – an island community away from the hustle and bustle of big city life. Geography offered a unique element for studying subjects as they were virtually isolated from many disruptive forces, offering unique controls for observation.

DOI: 10.4324/9781003162971-1

This study revealed that, as per conventional wisdom, high-risk life circumstances in early life often lead to a cycle of challenges later in life. Yet among the group, Werner found a significant proportion, about one-third of the high-risk individuals, who displayed resilience. Remarkably, they developed into caring, competent, and confident adults despite their troublesome developmental histories. They beat the odds.

What made this even more encouraging was that the evidence further revealed different stages for recovery. In other words, there was not a specific age or developmental marker that shuts down the possibility for recovery. Windows of opportunity opened throughout development. Different subjects showed surprisingly promising recovery in childhood, and beyond.

How was this possible and what can be done to arrange, if possible, the same safeguards for our ever-increasing community of distressed learners? Werner and Smith (2001) identified *protective factors* in the lives of resilient subjects, which helped them balance out risk factors at critical stages in their development. Among these factors were a strong bond with a non-parental caretaker (teacher, coach, mentor, etc.) and involvement in a social group, such as religious or other community affiliation. Much of Werner's work provided the foundation for later development of best practices in larger, less controlled settings, where most children reside within integrated residential communities.

Promising? Yes. However, the problem with much of this evidence was that it was not easily transferable to everyday classroom practices, for teachers, trained in content. Teachers may have had a basic developmental psychology understanding. Yet, they do not possess a comprehensive clinical background in trauma from extensive training in subjects like abnormal psychology.

That is where this text offers a solution; a promising and refreshing, practical approach to help teachers and educational leaders support children suffering the impact of trauma. As importantly, this text provides workable techniques for how to get children to persevere not just despite but often because of the difficult life circumstances they face in their young lives.

While scientific bases for effective practices matter and much of this text is based on scientific (as well as anecdotal) evidence, practitioners do not have the luxury of time to immerse themselves in technical training that clinicians receive training in. Those in the trenches, in classrooms across America and beyond have at the core an expectation to fulfill, and that is to help students achieve academically. These performance gauges are not often measured in emotional wellness. Yet emotional wellness must always be soundly centered for learners to excel. This field guide vows to assert the value of wellness and provides the guidance, a roadmap to chart the course in aiding children in the greatest need.

This text is written with the practitioner in mind; the busy educator who needs fast yet effective tools to aid children in their social development, especially when their development has been inhibited by trauma. The recognition that educators spend more time with students than any other adults outside the home, including counselors and therapists further supports the need to enlist these strategies and techniques. The symptoms of trauma are too great and the reasons too complex for teachers to delve deeply into scientific theory. Best practices are offered while framing this important context.

Increasingly, events both broadly and more locally have increasingly thrust trauma into the spotlight, and that is not a bad thing. In an era of expanding uncertainty, we should tune into to the true nature of student challenges, and leverage these as opportunities to inspire and support all learners who are under duress from risk factors. Motivated by those that rise to the occasion to assist, we often see an outpouring of love and support in times of crisis. Dedicated support can, if properly approached, truly support children who face the daunting hurdles of trauma.

Educators who develop a plan organized around a reckoning that traumatic experiences endured by students will position them to connect and help these children to achieve. Teachers can more adeptly frame their methods for aiding children and help them succeed far beyond expectations. Throughout this book, case studies and scenarios will be provided to characterize scalable methods and how to administer them, quickly and efficiently.

As school communities navigated their way through events that revealed the trauma from a once in a lifetime pandemic in the year 2020, and racial equality issues escalated onto the national scene, exposing a harsh view of inequities, we were reminded of how vulnerable these events make children and, for that matter, adults. The fragile nature of the circumstances surrounding stability in our world continue to shift. This changes how we can and should view teaching and helping children.

We can embrace opportunities to nourish the growth of children in the face of their personal challenges that cause distress. After all, trauma and post-traumatic stress are often pointed out as causing severe, even disabling conditions in children. Recognizing this now, more than ever is a testament that it is time to act, in a strategic manner, and in such a way that effectively reverses this cycle.

Consider a different perspective: for every child who has experienced post-traumatic stress, there are some who have experienced post traumatic *growth*; the ability to grow and excel because of their trauma, not despite it. Many inspiring stories abound in invigorating ways that show us, with courage and hope a way out, a better outcome. Leveraging a challenging experience conveys the message that through productive struggle, children can persevere, prevailing against the odds. In fact, acute forms of trauma can even enable them to grow through and from this experience.

We often hear the accounts of heroes like Olympic athletes, whose stories about overcoming the odds seemed insurmountable. These are often rooted in their fight against traumatic obstacles Integrated into the roadmap provided in this text are various accounts of successful counter punches; ways people found to fight back. Further, the user of this text can treat it as a guide, to shape and accelerate their opportunities to impact traumatized learners. It is not an end all but rather, a way to navigate, with several options to choose from to get to the end point. This guide is complimentary to clinical supports, rather than a replacement for them.

Teaching and leading schools matters more than ever, and this is heightened by how traumatic events, whether they be localized and personal, or broad and global, are a part of kids' lives. The reader should consider how to prepare themselves with the resources, tools and most of all, road maps to guide their route toward helping children and their families. The goal is to help families in ways that they too can strive through, beyond, despite, and perhaps because of their inevitable challenges. Accepting this as our reality is the first step in truly helping children move beyond the effects of their trauma.

Implementing steps to guide practitioners serves as the guardrails that can aid our students. The resources provided are derived from a research base and anecdotal, experiential resources, of over 20 years of the author's work with distressed children. One educational leader recalled his first day teaching in a combined autism and behaviorally disabled classroom. A child entered who had just been physically abused by his intoxicated mother. No college training program prepares beginner teachers to handle circumstances like this, and certainly not to treat their trauma.

Legal obligations often take precedent in urgent circumstances like this one, and often at stake is covering the school. That is important but do not lose sight of the child, who will not simply and suddenly recover with a cheerful, "welcome" greeting and smile. Instead, look at the practical approaches, short and long term, which will be offered throughout.

That young teacher had months to reach this child. He finally did, with patience and intuition. Yet if he had had access to this guide, it could have taken much less time and been more impactful. Experience is a part of this plan. Time-tested practices are vices for aiding students as they find ways to overcome their ever-increasing challenges. This happens both in a child's own day-to-day life, and in the world around them.

Developing a coordinated plan helps to frame methods for aiding students, and guides them to succeed beyond expected performance, as illustrated in the scenarios integrated throughout this text. These examples provide tangible, real world and scalable methods educators can apply quickly as a resource, right from a finger on a page of this guidebook.

A successful process for implementation must be concrete, applicable regardless of resource limitations, and available across the diversity of landscape that represents our nation's schools, and broad educational institutions. As previously mentioned, there is no silver bullet contained within this text, nor a prescription that fits precisely into your school, as if to apply an exact method for success. Roadmaps do not account for traffic jams and accidents happen along the way. Yet there are always ways around these obstacles, to the endpoint. Implementing flexible methods affords this kind of navigation flexibility.

The practitioner who adapts methods, applies them step by step, and commits to these, while balancing the necessary adjustments is more likely to help many children recover, much of the time. Doing so in a manner that adapts to the practitioner's circumstances, school culture, and context are critical That is why one of the major considerations in this book calls on you to apply each step within your school's unique framework. Not mine, nor your cross-state colleagues, but yours. To work, it must be authentic to your community, not serve as a commercial endorsement.

Educators often struggle in their caring demeanor with a desire to save everyone, rather than accepting the greater likelihood that "most of their students, most of the time" can succeed. Indeed, we became educators because we wanted to help all students. We strive to reach all children. We are nurturers, serving as surrogate parents who endeavor to believe in every one of our precious students, including the vulnerable.

These are the ideals that led us to teach; to not give up on any child, under any circumstance. Over time, we may have become jaded at the dim outlook of some of our learners. This happens in challenging environments, where the odds may seem insurmountable, or in communities struck by economic devastation or other hardships. The reality is that at-risk populations such as impoverished and racial minorities continue to face discrimination, often the result of "unintended microaggressions;" those unaware that their subtle behaviors contribute to the inequity.

Because educators entered a field believing that they must refuse to give up on any child, they can become disappointed by the end results, when even just one fails. Instead of expecting perfection, we should reframe our thinking regarding our commitment for improving the odds with children in need of help. That is our calling. Why not consider increasing the opportunities that children can and will succeed, on a scale, rather than an end all, of success or failure?

Consider the plight of 100 students. A standard bell curve suggests that approximately one-third of them will struggle to succeed, while another third of them would be ok, and that the top third will excel beyond expectations (Sherrington, 2017). Wouldn't it be inspiring to change the direction of that bell curve and increase the odds? Nudging the numbers over to the right, the side where more success is demonstrated as a path to success would be far more encouraging than an end all, of success, or failure.

If you looked at that random sample of 100 students across a school system, and knew these odds, how would you feel if you could alter the trajectory of the bottom third of the bell curve, and eliminate perhaps half of those low performers? Granted, there are still children who will continue to struggle. Yet this growth change is a motivator for educators and the challenge to cut that number, even in part, is well worth the commitment to apply tactics that will help. Patterns of persistent resistance can shift to patterns of upward trajectory, not in whole, but as a broad overall trend toward a direction of success. That is progress.

Outlined in this book are three strategic processes, intertwined into a blueprint that together creates a more synergistic approach to fostering student success, as they work to excel beyond their distress. References to traumatic events serve to represent a large sample of impacted students, and the way in which we can attack problems that children may encounter. Creating this synergy takes each one of these ideas, coordinated together, and fosters a compound effect created by combining, or stacking, them in a cumulatively influential methodology.

The strategies outlined are not necessarily ordered steps, although more acute student challenges should be addressed first, before initiating others and proceed along a continuum. These stages are tracked alongside each other. In other words, "stacking" these methods together puts in motion a proactive approach that will work for many, not all, in ways that illuminate this synergy. 1+1+1 = greater than 4, in this case. By implementing these together, we multiply exponentially the benefits received by our students.

Practitioners who apply one or two of these steps can certainly increase the potential to help a child to succeed beyond their obstacles. Yet combining and phasing all three parts together in and out at approximate intervals, potentiates a network of greater and greater possibilities for success. You can visualize these flowing in and across each other as the child is exposed to each (Figure 1.1). For our students' sake, this tactical approach and the time and resources invested in them are well worth implementing.

This text proposes a practical way to address these interconnected components in a child's overall recovery and growth as a learner. First, the state of wellness of the child must be

**FIGURE 1.1** Three-Part Cycle of Phasing

Credit Line: Antonia Germanos

examined. We must recognize the potential for trauma through identifying the signs. Second, data collection from frequent micro-formative assessments is to be gathered, organized, and utilized to inform the practitioner. This must happen while not inundating the child with exhaustive and lengthy assessments. Thoughtful caution in implementation at this phase is necessary as an overabundance of these all at once can be traumatizing to a child, in their own right.

Finally, inspiring your once traumatized students to set meaningful and practical goals as they lay out a path toward long-term, sustainable growth and success increases the likelihood of the ultimate goal to achieve. Practitioners can practically aspire to help children reach this through a calculated path as outlined in this guidebook. The text further allows educators to instill a prescription that is manageable for each individual child, knowing that reaching many (if not all) of your students will increase their success, with adaptability for course corrections.

Experiencing broadly traumatic events has overwhelmed the resources of school communities, as they navigate with caution, through threats, and repurposing for how to teach and educate around and through these predicaments. Events in, around and beyond school communities present understandably distressing experiences and when a stressful event has occurred, we must turn our attention to how we return the child to school, safely and successfully.

We can further use this as a longitudinal road map for individual and in large-scale trauma in the future. Using the three-step process, here is how:

1. <u>Start with high interest, rapport building opportunities</u>: cultivate relationships early and often. Remember how important icebreakers were? Multiply that value by ten. Remember, kids return to school with less structure, and greater challenges as they arrive to a new school year, and more so from a recent traumatic experience. It is sometimes hard to imagine how impacting this can be.

The effects of trauma can be far more impactful than we adults, distracted by our own demands of standards requirements, classroom management expectations, and curriculum guidelines, are often able to stop and notice. This is not an indictment on teachers, rather a recognition and step forward. We cannot ignore this. We must embrace and leverage this recognition for the benefit of our students. Do this strategically by embracing the progressive nature built in here.

Here are a few tips:

a) Prompt kids about what they learned from a recent challenge, especially the kind that may be beyond their control. How did they struggle with this experience? How if possible, did they benefit from it? Did they get to learn more about themselves or someone else? Did they gain a greater appreciation for friendships or learn through disappointment? Did they discover something new, about themselves, the world, or their school? This has the advantage of putting the attention on the child, and at the same time, encourages them to reflect about their circumstances in new, objective, constructively critical, and thought-provoking ways.

b) Offer kids perspective about large-scale traumatic events. For instance, you can show them the statistics and data on how the 1918 pandemic was tragically worse than the pandemic of 2020. Stage this in a game format, such as a trivia tournament. Think of fun, competitive online activities that trigger high interest, such as games like Kahoot. This and the ability to extrapolate data on students from gamification can be expanded into a social studies, literary, or science activity later on.

c) Just have fun with them. Ask them to share a humorous experience they encountered or have them recall an unforgettable event, such as when they were shuttered into safety with their family during quarantine, or an online video experience. Maybe their grandma had her camera positioned straight up her nose; or perhaps the family pet did something laughable.

d) Do not dismiss the sheer reality that some children may be returning from trauma bearing tremendous burdens that persist. Children, like adults, express their trauma in different ways. This makes the practicality to gauge the degree of impact for some, difficult to appear on the surface. This matters and educators must be prepared to support children suffering from the weight of wide-ranging trauma, with counseling and other trauma-related services that will be offered here.

2. Give a lot of small, incremental assessments: This may sound counterintuitive to the first, icebreaker/relationship building approach, as you worry kids will react with anxiety from the demand of evaluating their skills, "Oh no, I'm dealing with all of this and you're already making me take tests on top of it?" Let us examine how you can strategically conduct these, extending their learning while gaining a firm understanding of the child's readiness to take on their challenges.

First, think tactically. Do not usher in a two-hour assessment and expect this to work, or to engage students, let alone help you to gain authentic data on student progress. Implement smaller, thoughtful formative assessments. Sprinkle your mini assessments in compact, regular doses.

There is a tremendous body of research that reinforces that small, formative assessments offer reliable and predictive ways to measure student success, at least as, or even more effectively than, larger summative measures, and at the same time, reinforces learning (Berwick, 2019; Educational Data Systems, 2018; Brame & Biel, 2015; Dunlosky, Rawson, Marsh, Nathan, & Willingham, 2013).

Second, do not present this as a pop quiz surprise, or students will groan with anguish and dismay ("Oh no, not again. Why does she have to surprise us like that?!"). This has the psychological effect of a "gotcha" mentality on students. Instead, use opportunities like social awareness bonding and perspective building as ways to strategically connect students and gain information.

For instance, comparisons between the civil rights movement of the 1960s and modern-day efforts to institutionalize equity, illustrate a hopeful world, narrowing gaps between the privileged and underprivileged, serving as literary opportunities. Or perhaps in math, when calculating the numbers to equalize for all as a data set comparison that represents a way to demonstrate the differences. These are relevant to students and are meaningful ways to implement as learning opportunities within the content areas.

Third, as Lahey (2014) suggests, some of the best, most genuine assessments are those that are quick and inform the teacher concisely about student progress. These offer robust data sets that reveal learning potential for students. Think of Do Now introductory activities, following the prior day's lesson, or an exit activity at the end of a lesson or unit. Even gamification exercises to review comprehension for students offer valuable response data information, as the abundance of online learning games and tools are increasingly accessible, and data can be captured from them. Examples of numerous online gaming tools will be discussed in greater detail later in this text.

These real-time assessment activities offer an accurate if not informal account of the child's current understanding of skills, and are sharply focused on one or two proficiencies, not a battery of broad-based knowledge sources. Incrementally administering these is both subtle, and cumulative because over a week, or a pre-established sequence of time, you can quickly evaluate a half dozen or more student proficiencies. Extrapolating this data progressively provides a surprisingly larger and more tangible exhibition of performance data that the practitioner can use to make informed decisions in support of a student's recovery and growth.

Use technology to accumulate micro-data on student progress. Leverage tools like Google or Microsoft forms from student activity responses. Short mini assessments also make room for you to examine a student's understanding in shorter time intervals, such as a weekly time frame. Then provide the support needed either individually, or in small groups to your students during the mid-section of your lesson (or week) as you manage a trajectory of data collection intervals.

Utilizing short-term probes is a viable way to develop a knowledge base for your students' readiness levels. This approach is far less invasive to the well-being of children, a factor emphasized in point one of the three-step process and at the same time, provides at least nearly as accurate a picture of the child's aptitude. At the same time, this process increases retention of skills learned, as documented in the premise that shorter, more frequent formative assessments help students to retain their learning acquisition more effectively than longer ones.

3. <u>Challenge students to set goals just above their current level of ability and slightly outside of their comfort zone,</u> so achievable, progressive outcomes are produced. When individuals are challenged just beyond their comfort level, they are motivated to achieve. This slight elevation in tasks can be visualized by the student in a manageable way. Students can literally "see" and access this more tangible level of rigor, like the next step on a staircase, rather than one on the other end, hundreds of feet away, over the horizon. Additionally, learning just above one's capacity is typically more motivating when experiencing the development of skill sets.

So, what is "just above the comfort level," and how do you measure and determine it? Classifying this in some way depends considerably upon the child, and the context. Some children may need to move slower, more cautiously, at least at the start. Achieving a task often propels the learner to seek out the next milestone, or experience, and if they have gone this far, they are likely to desire just another step further . . . and another.

When asked what a slightly above comfort level barometer is for seemingly ordinary people who have been shown to achieve remarkable results by stepping into a highly focused, deep, "flow state," Steven Kotler, author of *The Rise of Superman* (2014) and *Stealing Fire* (Kotler & Wheal, 2018), provides a compelling answer. He refers to "The 4% Rule." That is, going 4% outside of your comfort zone is safe enough, not too distant to visualize and allows the learner to feel the incremental, progressive success, however small, moving in a steady upward direction.

The 4% Rule is truly an anecdotal and subjective concept, albeit backed by less proven, yet convincing, evidence. However, that is where the power of discretion by teachers provides for some insight and understanding into the concept. My 4% will be different from your 4%. In fact, it should be. The whole point of a number like 4% is that it is not a whole lot, and it is visible and within reach.

A small percentage higher is not overwhelming. Therefore, you are challenged to push just outside, into a new realm, but one where being able to step back into safety is not too far off in the distance. Too wide a gap further reinforces the very trauma students are challenged with. So where do we begin with helping a child to start at a place that is just outside their norm? How will we know? As significantly, how will we get them willing to do so?

Students can craft goals along a continuum that sets the stage for achievable, incremental levels and re-evaluate these regularly, following the mini assessments collected by their teacher to measure progress. Fulfilling these reachable micro assessments allows for small wins, victories that are quick, felt immediately and authentically by the student and are progressively motivating. This matters incredibly as related to the well-being and confidence of our students. Here, you see success perpetuating further success, small yet significant and steady.

Small wins equip the learner with critical skill development for persistence, and as important, enable the fortitude to keep going with resilience. While this is the result of achieving small and measurable milestones within the framework of assessment, it is linked closely to how students feel about themselves and therefore, with the management of their wellbeing necessary for them to push past their trauma and into growth and development.

Surprisingly, there is very little research regarding small wins, regarding the power to influence students' success. Much of the attention on small wins is in the corporate and self-help world. This lacking recognition of small wins psychology in the literature, would seem highly relevant for children, especially for those with challenges to overcome, like trauma. Yet a major void existed when researching for this text. References to existing literature to propose small wins and their intrinsic value in aiding children in the context of related programs and these outside examples will be proposed as a major tenant in the three-stop process.

Additionally, applying this in the context of student-centered support, alongside the fostering of relationships through fun, engaging experiences, and frequent, short term data collection has the appeal of working synergistically. Rather than serving as standalones, which would not net the same impact, combining these together increases the likelihood of success. Continuing to build on this concept will allow the practitioner to gain knowledge of exponential growth in her learners as they take a path not despite their trauma but learning to access their strengths because of and through it.

Striking this steady, just above the mastery threshold and accessible balance is highly invigorating and sustainable for learners. They begin to internalize, especially with their wellness and data awareness points attended to, that they are close enough to work toward achieving their desired goal range and that is worth investing in to discover this balance.

Kotler (2014) refers to a state of "flow," in which the learner finds the sweet spot, between apathy and uneasiness. Learning is interesting enough in this space to encourage a nudge, a push upward. Like a rubber band, this can only be pushed so far before it breaks from the increased tension. Too soft and the rubber band does not serve its purpose of binding together these steps.

The zone of flow stands at a level that is not too high, allowing the motivated learner to experience a sense of growth in steady increments as he strives for achievement at his threshold. Fueling this slightly outside the comfort zone space can serve as the catalyst to spark an ideal level of production, initiated by a strong desire and motivation to keep going.

This gap between a challenge that is just within reach, and the learning experience that is at least interesting enough to maintain a high level of attention is an ideal space for growth to occur. This happens alongside and often because of the positive direction a child is exploring. It is in this space that both learning and the social-emotional fortitude for students to succeed in can surge.

Earlier this millennia, numerous authors presented the concept of shorter, steadier successes leading to a path of success and achievement, something predominantly based in the corporate world. In the Compound Effect, Hardy (2012) laid out a course of action that would yield remarkable results for an individual, by making small successive decisions. These would take the person to a desirable position in life. Every choice will result in a behavior, which becomes a habit. This blueprint outlined a step-by-step operating principle which when multiplied out, results in a magnitude of success.

Similarly, in the Slight Edge, Olson (2013) advocated for building upon accumulating successes, those organized around attitudes and actions, which were caused by a focus on responsibility and discipline, driven by defined values. When guided by this formula, success starts out small, and gains momentum, accelerating as if moving faster and faster down a steep hill.

The distinctively notable parallel between these two texts provides a historical perspective for the validity of small, steady developments in the right direction resulting in remarkably positive outcomes. What is missing from the literature are applications to school-aged children and how to deploy this alongside other strategies to facilitate the change in definitive and constructive ways. Consider a visual representation: two directionally placed arrows, one moving upward and more sharply, when making productive choices. The other arrow, downward and at a roughly equal, sudden decline when unproductive choices are made.

If learning becomes too far a bridge to cross, fear pushes the learner over the edge, and effective learning becomes unsustainable. The burden distressed children carry meets the overwhelming reality that they also lack the cognitive maturity to process these challenges. The acute trauma a child is experiencing overtakes the learner, and primal instincts kick in. Never mind the ability to sort out the hypotenuse of an angle. The solution? Keep learning attainable for the child and give a lot of feedback. This will be outlined in further detail later in the book.

Traumatized children and adults alike are focused on survival first. Children must be situated even more delicately to support themselves. Stay within a cautious pliability of this critical achievement balance between too simple (causing apathy) and too difficult (causing stress), so that learners stay connected, and do not regress. This is sustained by making achievement attainable and feedback-driven.

Think about a time when you were pushed far beyond your own ability to grasp a skill, or to master content. This likely caused a great deal of anxiety, and was counterproductive, setting you back to an earlier stage in your learning. You regressed. Pushing students over the edge, too far is debilitating and detracts from the three-step process contained in this guide; a path that can serve as the foundation for moving children beyond their trauma.

Therefore, using a formative data collection process becomes vital in developing a strategic path, one that does not push the learner so far over the edge that they stop in their tracks and revert to an earlier stage of their development. Faced with this unsustainable pressure, it is no wonder learners are inclined to procrastinate, and find ways to avoid altogether.

Practitioners are encouraged to remain vigilant in finding a balance to instill in students both a sense of hope and curiosity.

Likewise, it is important to refrain from "watering down" content in such a way that makes it less interesting and less challenging. Always nudge students to the just-above-the-ability-level sweet spot, as in Kotler's 4-percent barometer (2014).

Like great coaches in sports, always prod the level of comfort, gently and continuously. Small wins are powerful ways to gain access to a sense of confidence and progress. Start tiny, celebrate these micro-wins alongside your learners, and use them as a foundation to motivate students to move on a path to the next level of their development.

Employing the three-step process will encourage your students in effective and strategic ways that are coordinated to condense manageable approaches for them as they transition in their growth. It does not assert to solve every problem brought on by something as daunting as the macro and micro life events that impact a child's ability to function and thrive.

Rather, the three step process helps to smooth the transformation that must be confronted by hundreds of thousands of educators in providing a foundation for students to successfully navigate their trauma. Subsequently, this enables students to achieve in ways that help them to reach their potential, through resources and supports provided within this systematic process. This guide will provide the tools for that to be accomplished.

## Chapter Summary

This chapter introduces the challenges, considers current realities such as an increasing recognition over the past decade regarding the impact of student trauma, and enters the new world order of countering current and emerging challenges. The introduction offers a three-part method for addressing student trauma, and how to help students grow from it:

1. Start with fun, relationship building activities – consider their state of wellness.

2. Give numerous small formative assessments to gauge their current performance state and to make it manageable in small doses (regular exit or DO NOW activities geared toward checking for understanding). Continue to build and track this informal data.

3. Challenge students to set goals just above their current ability/comfort zone.

# 2

# Recognizing Trauma in Learners, Macro and Micro

Before we can treat the trauma that students endure, we must first diagnose it. Trauma should be examined from both a macro and a micro lens, large scale and individualized. This is because students do not telegraph their trauma, as if to knock on the classroom door and announce, "I have experienced trauma and am requesting your assistance." In fact, some of the escape mechanisms students may use serve as a protective layer to shield them from perceived danger.

Even if students are appealing for help, they may not be doing so in a well-contrived way, even if they are not presenting as being "just fine" to mask the true challenges they encounter. Not acknowledging trauma is in fact a coping mechanism, even as it has long-term negative effects. Differentiated responses by children surface, and understanding this underlying diversity in student reactions helps us tune into their unique underlying issues.

This is especially true when the trauma is so raw, so acute, that for some children developing coping mechanisms to numb the pain may seem better, at least in the present, then enduring

DOI: 10.4324/9781003162971-2

the chronic and devastating pain of trauma. Unfortunately, this does not properly treat the injury. The trauma lurks deep beneath and can surface at a moment's notice, at perhaps the most inopportune and unexpected times, further inhibiting any progress made. Think about moments of unpredictable behaviors or outbursts. These may indicate an underlying stress, a deeper seeded trauma.

It is helpful for educators to approach students as likely being traumatized rather than assume that they are socially healthy, until ruled out, or disproven through a vetting process. In this way, a heightened sensitivity can aid in both sensing the problem under the potentially camouflaged layers, and of approaching the challenge with the likelihood that trauma exists in some form from a proactive mindset. Certainly, approaching children with the kind of empathy and care that presumes duress will not hurt the untraumatized child either.

## Methods for Identifying, and Creating Safe Spaces for, Student Disclosure of Trauma

Mindfulness Rooms for identification and treatment:

Consider setting up a structural framework for students to manage emotions, such as a place of tranquility and safety; a mindfulness room. This kind of resource aids everyone, even the least traumatized. Access to a safe space room can be most especially helpful to the profoundly impacted. So, make this resource available to all. For those who benefit from it most, have immediate access to a secure, structured school setting. For everyone else, even common school ailments like test anxiety can be a temporary challenge that warrants support mechanisms from the likes of a mindfulness room.

A mindfulness room serves as a safe space, one in which children begin to open up and this is where the identification of a problem can be initiated from. Some may be critical of instituting a room like this for presenting the view that enabling soft skills and allowance for children to manipulate and use an escape like this room is to get out of something. While this may be a legitimate concern, it does not bear the rationale to dismiss the benefits of a safe space in schools, especially for those in dire need of such emotional supports.

Consider the effects that many children have been confronted with, and based on these sometimes-tragic circumstances, warrant the need to be proactive, rather than reactive to the problems that students face from trauma. One school refers to their mindfulness room as the *Zen Den*. It is a place of refuge, a sanctuary, where kids benefit from being able to open up and be supported onsite for their challenges, be it a daily distress or something far more deep-seeded.

## Characteristics of Mindfulness Rooms

Mindfulness rooms may sound resource heavy or time consuming to arrange, like a spa with overpriced scented candles, music equipment to broadcast pleasant melodies, cozy chairs, and manipulatives to affect the tactile senses. Yet mindfulness rooms can be constructed on a dime, and at little time expense, too. Let us consider how, and what tools we can use to support the foundation of a safe space for all children to have access to when they need it. We will also examine when children are most likely to self-disclose their challenges in safe spaces.

Since ambient noise can have a soothing effect on our physiology, invest in Bluetooth speakers, at a minimal cost of $5. These inexpensive speakers can be paired up to any digital device that plays music from free resources, like YouTube. This is a cost-effective way to bring pleasant ambient background noise to your mindfulness room. Search online for *mindfulness music*, or *spa music*, and you will quickly find hours of sounds. Keep in mind that this should remain at a decibel level that is not too soft, nor too loud. The best is around 70 decibels.

This is something that can be easily measured with a phone or computer app: simply search online for a *decibel meter* for any device you have access to. This ideal background noise level has the advantage of serving up a distracted focus to the senses. That is, students are distracted away from the frenetic disruptions of the outside world, yet not so much that their higher executive thinking is disrupted. At this level, they are able to sustain a peaceful focus.

## Lighting

We have all woken up from a deep slumber as the sun peers through broken curtain coverage or someone suddenly beams bright lights onto our waking, struggling eyes. This does not only affect the eyes, which are placed close to the brain, working as acute sensors; lighting affects our wellness as a direct path to our neural pathways. When we cannot access natural light by being inside, arrange soft, sensual lighting inside. Harsh and bright lighting has an adverse effect, increasing a person's anxiety. We want to be aware of how lighting is staged in a wellness room for the best mood and affect.

Replace brighter, standard bulbs with a softer tone in your mindfulness room. Lighting has become more efficient and better quality while not cost prohibitive. Yet many schools have ancient lighting systems that cannot be substituted, due to their institutionally constructed and aged lighting systems. In these settings, simply cover bright lights with white paper, or light-colored shaded paper. Do not make it so dark that people will be stumbling into your room. Just soften the lighting, so that visual receptors are facing less harsh, more pleasant conditions.

## Chairs

Sitting in a comfortable position is an important part of providing the comfort that draws our students into more open conditions regarding their ability to express their needs and causes of distress. This is an additional reinforcement for a foundation that fosters safe spaces for children, both to reveal their concerns and to reduce tension from them. Comfortable chairs are most likely a pricier commodity on your accessory list when designing your mindfulness room, so consider the following options.

Expensive aerodynamic chairs may be out of reach for a school's limited budget. However, neighborhood big box stores and franchises such as Walmart, Target, and furniture chains are often willing to donate a few items like this to promote their product and good will. See letter in Appendix A as a sample pitch of your request for their support of our efforts to help children in need. Corporate offices may also be giving away the last generation's model, and removing old furniture for them is an easy draw for a big, busy corporate entity.

Chairs can also literally fit students' need for comfort. More will be discussed about "right-sized" or flexible seating in a subsequent section. For now, understand that students may benefit from settling into their comfort zone with the chair that best suits them. Many children may prefer a beanbag. Others may like a "zero gravity chair." Still others may prefer a bungee chair, and many prefer a gaming type chair, as they are accustomed to this personalized style when at home. Illustrations of one school's chairs are in Figure 2.1.

## Tactile Objects

Children, especially those who are anxious, benefit from keeping their hands occupied, by manipulating and touching objects as a helpful strategy to alleviate their stress and anxiety. This can have the effect of addressing aggressive feelings and enables the person to literally "feel" as though they are taking control

**FIGURE 2.1** Flexible Seating

of something in their space. These objects are typically cheap and can be found at any $5 or bargain store.

Some typical examples of tactile objects include stress balls, a Rubik's cube, other squeeze toys, "chewelry," (something you can chew on which can wrap around your neck or wrist, kind of like a phone cord), Silly Putty, Koosh balls, and spinners. Of course, these may be too distracting to be in a classroom, but in a sanctuary like a mindfulness room, they fit perfectly.

## Fishtanks

Small fish tanks are inexpensive and visually pleasing to the eye. Think about a restaurant with that grand tank at the entrance. The bubbling water and tranquil eloquence of the creatures inside can truly put a person's mind at ease. Yet there is even more to the usefulness of a fish tank. Students visiting can effectively "adopt" the fish and care for the tank. Anyone who has managed the care of animals understands the need to maintain and clean the tank and care for the creatures. Taking care of another life is an effective therapy for many (not all) children. Take advantage of this fact by enlisting willing students.

## Mindfulness Resource Board

Resource or menu boards offer a series of sequential strategies, many of which are shared throughout this text. They include journaling prompts, mindful meditation guides, desk stretches, breathing tips, self-talk, and positive affirmations. Offering a menu to choose from like this allows users a choice in how they will manage their emotions, and that aids in the journey of taking back control. Since control is one of the critical elements needed for recovery of students impacted by the effects of trauma they feel negligent in, any control technique can be beneficial. Figure 2.2 refers to an example of one such resource board.

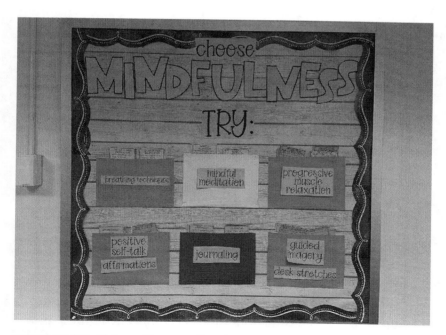

**FIGURE 2.2** Mindfulness Resource Board

## What's on the Wall? Powerful Subliminal Messages

Well-displayed messages can set a tone and send a message to guests. These can be simple statements, like the affirmations mentioned earlier. While motivational illustrations can and should be displayed throughout an entire school building, they matter even more in a wellness or mindfulness room, where healing can occur, with positively reinforcing statements serving as sublimation therapy.

Think of the warm welcome you feel at a well-run business, like Disneyworld; aesthetically pleasing restaurants, where powerful messages help us reframe our mindset; or locker rooms, where teams strengthen their resilience to win. This is even smart to post on an exit door, so that students are not just entering to welcome messages but are also being reminded of this on the way out, as shown in Figure 2.3.

## Framing Your Situation – How Do You Feel Prompts

Like positive affirmations, self-inquiry questions can stimulate self-reflection. Students should be honest with themselves about how they feel, and what is bringing them to their current state of mind, before they can begin to address their emotions, and reverse destructive cycles with positive self-talk strategies. Examples like the one in Figure 2.4 are simple, clear, and get kids actively thinking constructively about their own internal conflicts and challenges. This can get them to open up, and that's the first step in identifying the need.

Student trauma can be a complex process, and therefore, trained psychiatrists are certainly best equipped to serve as diagnosticians. Yet trained psychiatrists are not typically on the front lines, helping students to self-regulate and manage their emotions, in classrooms for seven or more hours a day. Educators are those at the center of managing students and the symptoms of their challenges. Trauma has wide-ranging manifestations in student responses and responding with tools of the trade in the moment is a significant factor in recovery efforts.

**FIGURE 2.3** P.S. You Got This

This guidebook does not propose to transform educators into trained clinicians, ready to diagnose and provide therapy to students' long-term and intrinsic symptoms. Rather, teachers should look to this text for ways to recognize the wide-ranging signs of trauma as opposed to assuming a child intentionally

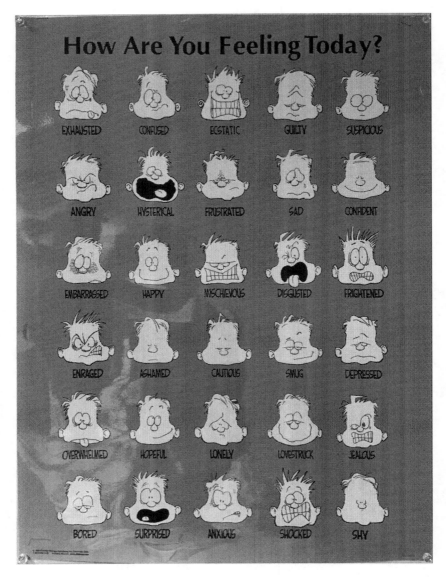

**FIGURE 2.4** How Are You Feeling Today?

misbehaves, shuts down or shows off, resulting in being referred to the office. Additionally, having a repertoire of strategies to respond with is a win-win. Supporting children with a keen eye makes the management of class and lessons much more feasible.

Once a teacher identifies signs a child is faced with the symptoms of trauma, they can be better equipped to use this information to aid him. Beginning with this awareness, educators may be better prepared to respond very differently than conventional means to aberrant student conduct, resulting from the impact of sustained distress.

Traditional methods can be stubbornly held onto by individuals without the resources of a manual to guide the way. Yet one thing is clear: conventional methods no longer serve a functional purpose. Part of the process for enabling teachers to support traumatized learners is providing them with a sound understanding of their student's behaviors and knowing where to look regarding options that exist for selecting a feedback method.

Many educators have become familiar with buzzwords, phrases like *restorative justice*. In some murmuring circles, the perception is that providing a restorative justice model has become an "excuse," to allow misbehavior and permit kids to *get away with it*. This is one way of resisting approaches to managing student trauma. It is possible that students could be using interventions as an excuse, a way out. So what? We now know from years of research on school discipline how ineffective traditional approaches are (University of Michigan, 2018), so why not explore alternatives?

Here is another way to help teachers understand negative response patterns of students: traumatized children are not trying to get away with anything. Instead, the opposite is often true: they are escaping an unsettling reality and the tremendous pain associated with it. This is hard to see because it is not a physical wound, like a stubbed toe, or a brush burn that we can be sensitive to and put a Band-Aid on. Something we can *see* is what many educators and parents connect to. Putting a Band-Aid on a child makes the injury real, and treatable.

Remember that children often lack the skills and tools to manage their challenges. Why should we expect them to? Many adults struggle with these same qualities. For children, their brain has not physically developed the capacity to fully regulate in logical ways. Even a "normal" child experiences risk-taking behavior which result in consequences. The difference is the outcome of the risk for a typical child serves to act as enough of a deterrent to curb the behavior in the future. Their skill set is strong enough that they can adapt; they "learned their lesson."

Indeed, beginning with identification, educators should use research-based tools and time-tested practices, as outlined in this guide, not to *cure* a child, but rather to support treatment efforts; to help students learn the skills to manage the trauma and subsequently, their workload, more adequately. This text details ways to manage student trauma, anxiety, and stress and then to help children strive beyond it, with practices applied which are highly effective and not at the cost of time and resources.

Schools have improved in their understanding and implementation of techniques to support emotional development in children. Now, these techniques and resources need to be refined and used consistently, sprinkled in as a resource with greater depth for distressed learners. Certainly, combining them as multiple methods provides a vehicle, serving as a viable inventory of options. The synergistic effect resulting from students being exposed to multiple methods reinforces the three-step process highlighted in Chapter 1, helping students develop wellness, side by side along with monitoring their performance.

These resources do not require the acquisition of costly commercial products. At the same time, a variety of options are made available, since one size does not fit all. Like a group who sits in a restaurant and selects different menu items, students benefit from having and learning to be offered a variety of resources. Consider the options and add these together. Offering only one, or a limited resource set, may be too restrictive, and you will not be able to reach as many distressed students as you have the potential to.

Think of the theories regarding different learning styles. We do not teach all kids using the same approach, straight lecture, or just through presenting audiovisuals, or any other solo method, for that matter. Students are offered different ways to attack a problem, or learn the content. Why would we expect anything different from offering social-emotional resources to students? For instance, school counseling sessions as standalones do not serve to provide all encompassing aid for every child. Multiple options exist, especially those related to real, day-to-day life circumstances for a best fit with certain students.

School personnel should stock up on a set of tools, even as they are learning better ways to diagnose their students. Methods for identification should be simple, time-tested practices such as identifying the ABCs behavior therapy, a method that has been well established in working with students with greater cognitive needs. Consider a variety of options when you design your field based diagnostic instruments. Borrow from and adapt suggested options contained here. Remember, these options do not serve as an end all, but a good place to build a stockpile, while many resources remain at your disposal.

Antecedents, Behaviors, and Consequences (ABCs) is a mnemonic device that when put in play, can be helpful in addressing student issues on the fly. The following is the concept, well-established in special education literature and certainly well-suited to the current context for addressing students' needs who are impacted by social-emotional challenges from trauma, regardless of their cognitive ability level.

> *Antecedent* – record interactions and behaviors that precede a behavior which warrant consideration for the manifesting action that indicates possible impact by trauma-induced conduct.
>
> *Behaviors* – include only *visibly observed actions by the student*. Do not guess at internal states of their emotions. Be specific and concrete, maintaining an objective framework.
>
> *Consequences* – these are the results of the behavior, including verbal interactions from staff/peers, physical interactions

from staff/peers, and any type of accountability resulting from the behavior.

When implementing an ABC intervention, it is important to have a quick access tool to record data, because behaviors can and will happen unpredictably. Have this resource available in advance. Even if you do not need them right away, they are great anecdotal documents to track students' wellness with and are telling in longitudinal examination of student behavior patterns.

Keep the recording document simple. You are often jotting the ABCs on the fly, perhaps during a lesson transition or between classes and this should not be complicated. This can be a hard copy document or stored digitally. Creating an electronic format allows for easy retrieval and data runs later. Use charting at least until a pattern is established. Table 2.1 is a sample document you may wish to adopt and adapt.

Another resource to consider when collecting data is an observed behavior chart. This has parallels to ABC tracking, and ties back to the goal of small wins and goal setting for learners. Here is how it works:

A common behavior or pattern of disruptions is observed in a child.

**TABLE 2.1** ABCs Chart

| | | | _Student Name |
|---|---|---|---|
| Date | Antecedent | Behavior | Consequence |
| | | | |
| | | | |
| | | | |

A *baseline* is collected, which allows for an objective and unbiased collection of the data. In this way, the teacher confidentially gathers the data without the student's knowledge, avoiding inaccurate collection of data. Typical redirections can occur but nothing more explicit, or radically different. This allows for gathering reliable data patterns. Then the data is shared with the student, with candor in the form of a private mini conference. The teacher explains to the child, with a quick comment to "meet me after class," during homeroom or a routine conferencing session.

At the mini conference, the student is advised that in a sampling of ten minutes over a period of three or more classes/days within a week, he or she has exhibited, for instance, talking excessively seven times. Calculated over a traditional class period, this value equates to 28 disruptions over a full class – a significant disruption proportion. Establishing goal setting and small wins is a topic explored throughout this text. For now, consider that a child even just halving this number is a significant improvement. Most would agree this is realistic, not overreaching by demanding a decrease or, unrealistically, perfection. It is a viable objective to strive for and a welcome reduction for the teacher.

Bringing to a conscious level the behaviors children exhibit completely unaware, or at least the frequency and degree of their adverse behaviors, often triggers a level of awareness that can produce vast and quick improvements. Furthermore, this helps students set deliberate goals that support their success. Figure 2.5 is a sample observed behavior chart.

The psychology behind ABCs and observed behaviors is that teachers and their students can track behaviors in a pragmatic format and work together to reduce the adverse behaviors. Certainly, this means that student conduct needs to be replaced with appropriate alternatives, to fill the void or these behaviors will soon return in the absence of an alternative. Appropriate options will be explored in greater depth in the chapter on using data to implement strategy to change behavior.

| Observed Behavior Data Chart: | |
|---|---|
| Student Name_____ Teacher_____ | |
| Date_____ 10-minute baseline timeframe_____ | |
| Standing up | |
| Off task with class assignment | |
| Talking | |
| Other | |

**FIGURE 2.5** Observed Behavior Data Chart

Adverse Childhood Experiences (ACEs) scores are data collection techniques (Center for Disease Control and Prevention, n.d.) that are more relevant in their application for school counselors and clinicians to coordinate, yet they are useful for teacher understanding in the present context.

Application of ACEs from a counselor-support perspective is due to the confidential nature of sensitive information and disclosure laws across states and regions. Unlike ABCs and observed behaviors charts, where the teacher is gathering patterns of behavior data, ACEs digs much deeper into the direct challenges' children are facing due to their sustained traumatic life incidents. These circumstances are frequently, though not exclusively, connected to home.

ACE scoring is used to quantify the amount of adverse childhood experiences a student has accumulated over time. In a traditional ACE model, there are three main categories: abuse, neglect, and household dysfunction. You can see why this format is more appropriate for counseling and clinical services to engage in, rather than being substituted by a classroom teacher. Counselors embark on the ACE model from a trained perspective, bringing their training into the complimentary support mechanism.

Therefore, ACE scores are a valuable resource and should not be dismissed. Using tracking with this tool will not serve as a practical classroom mechanism but rather as a complimentary set of data on the child that can be useful for decision making. Awareness of this instrument is useful for classroom teachers to know about as they are administering their own three-step framework.

It has been established that trauma should be examined at both a large-scale level (macro) and a smaller, more individualized level (micro). Macro trauma results from major events, like a massive regional fallout, war, a global pandemic, and amidst a national reckoning on racial equity, including what occurred at the onset of the 2020s. These more recent events may not have been previously considered as profoundly important. Yet, in our fast-evolving world, we had a true global and national case study to appreciate how large-scale events can and do have an impact on students' lives in significant ways. In the absence of support, we are not equipped to help children recover.

Consider that a large-scale event can have a massive impact with repercussions for children far beyond our understanding and preparation for managing the effects of the event. Finally, the realization that no matter what, daily life has quickly transformed how we interact, socialize, and connect with others. Adapting to this evolving new normal, and the challenge to thrive in school, has serious consequences to adjust to. These all weigh heavily, socially, and emotionally on children. When you combine them, they are even more impacting on kids.

Any collection of these factors further reinforces a cycle of traumatic experiences. There exists clear evidence that those most impacted across each of the domains are families at highest risk (Garcia & Weiss, 2020), further increasing a chance of decline in social wellness and student performance. Equity then, is a factor in our quest to balance student access to opportunity.

While schools adapt to evolving needs in support of traumatized children, and as they take on the macro challenges described here, they must continue to act on the micro (individual) level too. No longer can schools act in silos about student developmental challenges. If we truly want to help children develop post-traumatic growth skills, they must move beyond the cycle that locks them into a future of struggle and failure, which in the process further inhibits a child's growth.

Arming teachers with the knowledge that confined and traditional approaches do not work, we must shift their focus to flexible tools which aid in implementing treatment and progress. Doing so increases the impact of executing methods, allowing for step-by-step sustained change toward both addressing a child's trauma and helping them progress in a form of recovery.

To prepare teachers effectively and efficiently, professional development resources and investing the time to inform teachers must be dedicated to the cause. Using this guidebook as a framework is a practical approach, a collection of resources containing three linked components to connect the dots. It suits the current and ongoing challenge and compliments a professional development program to steer administrators, teachers, and counselors in the right direction to gain awareness, collect data and construct a plan for each student in need of our help to grow and flourish.

## Chapter Summary

With the foundation laid for the challenges and proposed solutions to act on, Chapter 2 begins by introducing the overwhelming evidence both in research and anecdotal terms about childhood trauma. A strong case is made to develop a keen awareness that children are traumatized, be it due to challenges they previously encountered, will encounter, or are currently confronted with. With this framework in mind, historical methods are challenged for dealing with addressing student conduct in silos and the groundwork is established for compelling educators to foster a multi-pronged and strategic approach.

# 3

# Treating the Trauma – Resources and Teacher Sensitivity

With convincing evidence illustrated that trauma is everywhere, and that it is also not exclusively a bad thing that causes life long, permanent deterioration, methods for moving forward from recognizing childhood trauma can be examined and adopted. Management and treatment are proposed, whether they be individualized or broadly based, or both.

Although there is not a definitive order in addressing student trauma, it is sometimes best to begin with a whole scale outlook for children to safely explore their challenges. After offering this outlet, many students feel liberated to seek out more individualized support. As such, presentation of strategies in this guidebook are formatted to begin with larger scale methods for inviting children in need to accept help. This is followed by individualized methods for attention to support children. Again, this is not a precisely mandated order; rather it is a guide that can be loosely but effectively referred to.

School counselors should not be acting in isolation in the treatment of students with trauma. There are many resources

DOI: 10.4324/9781003162971-3

beyond the shelter of a school counselor's office that compliment, rather than reduce or replace the need for counseling support. These resources include both people and programs.

## I'm More Than Just That

The program is referred to by its original name, *I'm More Than Just That*. This project engages high school students in connecting with middle school children about the challenges the older students endured at their age. These are relatable challenges, often painful memories that the high schoolers experienced as a middle school child. These include challenges such as bullying discrimination, equity issues, and more.

This program is best characterized by its origin story, which also shows how the project came about its name and why it continues to invigorate strength and hope in so many children. The relevance for this program is even greater today and remains resilient due to its practical application for so many. Here is the process, told in the true story of how it came to be.

High schoolers visit the local middle school every year, to share their raw experiences about having faced bullying and/or discrimination. Children who struggle with everything from sexual identity, inequality, body image, religious and racial injustices, and many other challenges that inflict on a child's vulnerable identity are shared. Their portrayals are often intimate details, proofed by adults who oversee the program, yet they remain authentic and powerful.

High school children of all walks participate on stage, appealing to their younger peers, followed by engaging in one-to-one discussions with students who wish to visit with them at their choice after the assembly. The connections are inevitable because everyone shares in at least one of their diverse stories of challenge. The premise of this impactful and far-reaching event was born from a simple, yet powerful introduction by one speaker, who kicked off the event in 2014.

A high school senior came to the stage and did not stand behind the podium, nor did he give distance to his audience. Instead, he sat with his feet dangling over the front of the stage, as close as one could possibly be on stage to his audience. With torn up sneakers, dressed in jeans and a grungy t-shirt, he introduced himself by first name and announced, "I like pizza." The middle school audience responded with thundering applause of agreement. "I like playing video games." The audience continued with still louder applause. "I like hanging out with my friends." The clapping and cheering continued to escalate. "And I am gay."

Silence. After a seemingly eternal yet intentional pause, he added. "And I tell you that last part because I am so much more than just that." The audience was riveted and, almost as if dared, responded with thundering, endorsing, and boisterous applause. After his turn, one after another, teenagers stood on stage and shared their individual, authentic, and raw stories. Each time, they received affirmative endorsement by their middle school audience.

Hence, a powerful phrase was born in this school. *I Am More Than Just That* means something more to this community than just those six words. It is a symbol that no matter what, a child is something much larger, much more wonderful than one identifying feature. The program returns every year. It remains a student and faculty favorite, for all the right reasons.

Coupled with this presentation are sessions arranged to allow middle school students direct access to their older teen peers after and beyond the program presentation, conducted in a coordinated and confidential manner. Students, one by one, spend the entire morning visiting with their older mentors, engaging with high schoolers, sharing, and connecting in ways only possible between children. The unspoken bond of a connection that "someone finally gets what I never knew anyone could" is the breakthrough realization of many middle schoolers on that day.

The program works because it does not simply offer a powerful message that ends abruptly and subsequently burns out fast, as so many commercial programs do. It is strengthened by the follow up invitations and the bond building that occurs between older and younger peers.

These subsequent sessions are strategically placed as an open door to students when it is most timely to do so, immediately after the impact of the program has been experienced. This intentional approach preserves the power of the program and sustains an outlet for visiting students to connect with their younger peers. This is treatment that works, is free and powerful.

Programs like *I'm More Than Just That* work so well, not because they offer a miracle cure, or serve as an exclusive standalone solution to a complex problem. These events work best when combined, in a stacked format, with other layers of interventions to support children. *I'm More Than Just That* is powerful; it inspires your community to laugh and cry together in support of a mission to help all children. Add more ingredients to multiply that effect.

The only impediment to universal implementation of a program may be in conservative communities that are not ready to accept the challenges today's youth face. That presents an even more systemic problem than the trauma children endure and is beyond the scope of this text. However, in time it is hoped that all communities come to a reckoning and accept practical interventions relevant to today's child.

Developing programs like *I'm More Than Just That* requires effort, yet is manageable and best of all, cost efficient and resource effective. School communities are not paying outside production companies. This is an in-house performance and that is exactly why it is so connected, so relevant and persuasive. Here is a general roadmap for developing the program in any school community that is ready to embrace its power.

Step 1: Start early, in the fall – recruitment should begin in October. Engage your student services, positive behavior support program, or a teacher leader who runs a co-curricular program affiliated with student life (LGBTQ, a diversity committee, an Equity club, etc.) to recruit willing high school students. These are often students who were counseled to address their own challenges, so you already know them. Some will accept willingly, some will think about it, and some will say no. Eventually, you will recruit enough to make the program work. Ten is typically the magic number at the school where this thrives. Five to ten is plenty.

Step 2: Establish that the students will need to compose their thoughts, in a prepared format. Depending on their comfort and ability level, this can be drafted independently, or alongside a facilitating adult. Ultimately, all presentations must be vetted for appropriateness. Sharing their traumatic challenges is not an invitation for divisive messaging and letting the high schoolers know this early and often is an important feature of promoting an authentic, yet positive storyline of survival on stage.

Step 3: Have a deadline for composition of stories – the "pioneer school" makes the holiday season in December theirs. Arrange for the facilitating faculty member or members to sort out the student compositions. If something is inappropriate, do not be quick to eliminate it. Rather like an effective English teacher, guide the student's message to an appropriate, more authentic message. We do not want to take their message away. We want them to deliver it in the most effective and appropriate manner, while preserving the story of their challenge.

Step 4: Upon return from the New Year, meet with the students to have them prepare how they will verbally present their compositions. Some students prepare an outline to speak in a less scripted format, others need a word-by-word teleprompt. Both are fine. Do not box them in. Let them practice their presentation in a way that they are most comfortable with. Remember, this is their story, and it matters as much to them as to their recipients.

Step 5: Go through a dress rehearsal so you can have the kids practice and perform to estimate the length of the assembly program. You may have to go through this two to three times to get it right. It is well worth the investment and conveys value and investment to your young presenters. It does not matter when you do this. It can be done before, during, or after school. Just do it when you can get your group together. You can even use club time if that works.

Step 6: Promote your program. While this is not linear, you should be prepared to start your advertising campaign a month before. Schools are busy places, easily distracted by the day-to-day demands. Messaging this as a reminder is important optics for all to process and look forward to in anticipating the experience.

Step 7: Schedule and prepare for the day of the program. The pioneer school typically runs it at the end of February. This is often the part of the year when kids are declining or struggling to see an end in sight. The holidays are over, it is cold outside, and the end of the school year is far off in the distance. Hence, it is the perfect remedy for a difficult time of year, and for struggling kids. The pioneering school buys bagels for the presenters and welcomes them into their old middle school. The principal meets and thanks each of them individually, for participating and their brevity. They are ready to go.

Step 8: Introduce the presentations. The facilitator of the program introduces the concept to the middle schoolers and reminds them that these are real high school students, with real stories and challenges. Start with your bravest high schooler (you know who they are). They will lead the way and set the tone. The rest will flow once kids start hearing these authentic stories, identifying with, or knowing a friend or family member whom they can connect to.

Remember that this is a holistic program. It is strategic and serves as an invitation to students to bring their individual trauma securely to the table. There is no safer way than opening the door with older kids, often looked up to by their younger peers, aligned by the common bond of a strong connection. They see older kids as those who can understand them best.

*They went through that too, yet they seem ok, so cool!* This is often the refrain heard from struggling middle schoolers. They feel like a crack in the door provides enough of a gap, wedged open for the outlet they need to take what they have kept inside, or where they may have pondered a destructive path as the only option. This is a critical first step, a call for help. Utilizing this as a resource, schools never look back, as they recognize the value and power, part of the three-step process offered in this guidebook.

## Mentorship

Mentorship has shown sustained results; when instituted thoughtfully, mentoring produces profoundly positive outcomes. Traditional mentor programs offer positives, but they can be exhaustive, resource and cost heavy. The best solutions emerge from unique models at grassroots levels that are less intensive yet equally effective, such as the *Restorative Service Program*, which will be detailed next.

The Restorative Service program (RSP) offers children the opportunity to meet with a teacher not assigned to the youngster, in a voluntary manner to discuss an issue they were referred for and to focus on constructively forward-thinking solutions. The mentor-student relationship continues beyond the one and done intervention, as the mentor continues in a supportive role for the child. This offers a tremendous alternative to traditional, ineffective punishment-based models that are typically reactive responses to a student referred, like the ineffective execution of punishments such as suspension.

Restorative service can match your school's resources in your quest to align a viable mentor-student model. For example, in one school, they employed a new corps of retired police officers, serving as school security. The concept: engage law enforcement veterans in a positive, productive manner to work non-punitively with at risk children. This has considerable advantages, not the least of which is breaking the cycle of barriers between generations of families regarding perceptions about equity challenges and law enforcement.

Fostering relationships between retired law enforcement and children who may be at increased risk of engaging in behaviors that could land them in trouble now and later on is a major advantage. Yet the bigger payoff is how offering this non-punitive mentor support model teamed up with families fearing law enforcement disrupts a perspective of cycles. The purpose of this text is not to debate who is right or wrong in these complex situations. Rather, we insist on examining the trauma that children experience and fruitful measures to reverse this trajectory.

Consider this: a child can engage in positive interactions with an adult authority figure, often for the first time outside of their family, and do so positively. Additionally, this is possibly the first male role model they may interact with, as most school security personnel are male. The school that arranged this program almost never faced a refusal by a student or family to accept a proposition for a child to engage in this non-punitive measure to support their child in lieu of suspension. This is a win-win.

This is of consequence far beyond the removal of an ineffective disciplinary action. Earlier it was noted that decades of research prove suspension is not effective. Worse, it has larger damaging repercussions school wide (Eilers, n.d.). When families are given alternative non-punitive options, and a child meets with a supportive adult, that experience can have an impact that reverses perception and acceptance by one or more family members too.

Convinced law enforcement has a negative effect on their family, children meeting a security officer get to see instead a dad, a man, a person, a teacher, and most significantly, not the enemy. They share their experience, either explicitly or implicitly. Perhaps their body language implies greater comfort at school. Or they just tell someone in their family that the experience wasn't all that bad, and *this guy is pretty cool!*

Furthermore, a massive longitudinal study on a remote island in Hawaii showed that at-risk children could overcome their obstacles with one significant difference maker: a mentor (Werner & Smith, 2001). Positive adult engagement will be discussed further later in the text. For now, the objective is to underscore the value a mentor has on a child who likely faces the odds, and the distress associated with their obstacles.

Of course, a school cannot simply pronounce one day that they have employed a restorative service mentoring program and say, "good luck," to the adults assigned to help children. Training is required, and, the right personnel. We all know teachers that are sensational with children, including the most challenging, and others who we might cringe if our own child had to sit in their class. The same goes for school security personnel. Be sensible about who you employ in this program. If no such option exists, go to plan B.

Plan B: This option can be deployed in lieu of school resource personnel. It will be a more practical choice in many schools today because they may make use of a positive behavior or incentive-based program. If this is already in place, leveraging teachers trained to engage in the restorative service program is simple. Yet restorative service can operate as a standalone, and that is why it can be easily replicable; well worth every school exploring as a method for supporting children under duress.

One such school assigns teachers in lieu of a duty assignment to the school's positive behavior support in schools (PBSIS) program. This is a collaboration between the state of New Jersey and Rutgers University. It is based in research and offers interventions in lieu of or alongside lesser disciplinary measures to help aid troubled schools and children. PBSIS is utilized in a broad swathe of schools but has its historic roots in urban communities, where the success of it could not be ignored. This resulted in its expansion, across the state.

Teachers participate in the PBSIS restorative service program in much the same way the previously mentioned school resource officers do. The key element is that these teachers do not teach the child. It is important for them to remain unbiased, and grading interferes with objective decision making. Additionally, there is no associated accountability ("where's your homework?"), and the teacher serves as an adult ally, in strict support of the child, during the RSP intervention and beyond.

## Restorative Service Process

In either the school resource officer or duty assigned teacher capacity, the process is essentially the same. A student exhibits misbehavior. This may result in a bullying investigation, due to disrespect toward authority, or other inappropriate action that results in a referral to the school administration. The administrator issues the necessary (if applicable) disciplinary consequences and separately, recommends the non-punitive RSP intervention.

A faculty member who does not teach the identified student is assigned to meet with the child during the available/duty period. The assigned adult is given a summary of the infraction and uses a sample guide along with one of the corresponding activities at a time during the school day that the student has more flexibility and when the teacher is also available.

The teacher files the documents the student worked on in an archive. Monthly meetings are held to review these with the administration and RSP team to make recommended revisions.

## Goals of the Restorative Service Program

Provide a structured format to focus on the future proactively. Unlike discipline alone, which is done in a vacuum, RSP offers an alternative outlet, an intervention with a caring, unbiased, and supportive adult, an ally. Since a detention or suspension is often assigned without any follow-up component that can help an offender recognize their actions and how to respond in the future, students are not equipped with options to adjust to make better decisions in the future.

RSP encourages positive relationships for troubled children with authority figures. As previously mentioned, the students that receive repeated discipline have a negative association with authority figures. By increasing the opportunity for students to interact with adults in a positively structured environment that is separate from negative consequences, they can begin to develop more fulfilling relationships. This provides a resource for times when they may need to ask an adult for help in the future.

The teacher or security officer meets the student in a neutral location, such as the school's media center, introducing themself to the child. The adult allows a few minutes to get to know the student. It is for this reason that facilitators should be mindful of selecting the "right" kind of staff, ones who can quickly and effectively build rapport and forge a relationship.

Once rapport is established, the adult initiates the exercise for the RSP. A sample facilitator's guide outlines how the teacher administers the RSP. This guide is designed like a lesson plan, to allow the teacher to follow, with options to adjust based on the needs of the child. The focus of RSP is organized around respect, because this is something that can be universally connected to virtually all kinds of infractions committed (Appendix B for Sample Facilitator's Guide).

Mentoring programs like RSP work if they are well-designed and implemented. The program has the effect of aiming to address a child's trauma, without overtly announcing it to the student. Mentoring commits to young people that there is someone who cares about them, assures them that they are not alone in dealing with day-to-day challenges, and makes them feel like they are valued – all tenets of the positive effects of mentorship.

## Middles to Littles

Instituting a program for at-risk children that engages them with preschoolers as readers, such as one school's program aptly titled "Middles to Littles," can work to connect middle or high school children with pre-k children. This works remarkably well as an incentive-based program that attracts struggling learners to give to young children in a way that breeds confidence and a sense of value in something larger than themselves. Imagine a towering middle schooler, one perhaps viewed by others as intimidating, sitting with a class full of vibrant preschoolers, eagerly shouting their excitement about being read to by "that cool older kid."

This altruism, a sense of giving back, feeds the powerful psychological urge that shifts a person's viewpoint from lacking serious self-worth to something important, something special, and something bigger than they could have imagined. The feeling experienced by the middle school children when 18 excited preschoolers hang on their every word is so substantial, middle schoolers describe with pride in their own words the rewarding feeling they experience. *That felt great . . . I want to do it again . . . what do I have to do to go back. . . . can I pick someone else who needs this?* These themes echoed repeatedly.

Helpers high may sound like a gimmick or something too simple, or too hokey, yet we can think of it as a common positive outcome for the helper. Simply stated, after doing good for others, our physiological response produces hormones that reinforces the good deed, like a boomerang effect returning to the sender. It is a natural "high" that is designed to influence us to persevere. A secondary outcome of this is the confidence and sense of self-worth that comes with it. By increasing this sense of self, individuals who struggle with challenges and trauma can build resilience and strength around their own compassion towards another.

In the school from which Middles to Littles sprang, the initiative happened by accident when the preschool ran out of room and had to be moved to the middle school. The Middles to Littles program came to life in ways that have affected hundreds of preschoolers and dozens of adolescents in positive, contagious ways. It is worth sharing the story of one special young man, who was directly impacted by experiencing this shared opportunity.

He was a towering young man, over six feet tall. He came from the other side of the tracks, and teachers who did not know him would shake their heads as he whipped by down the hall, laughing too loud and moving too fast. Yet behind all that was the ear-to-ear smile of someone who could offer so much more. When he was first recruited, the teachers leading the program did not know if he would just laugh and walk away or accept the invitation to read reluctantly. He did neither.

When he first entered the preschool classroom, the four-year-olds spiritedly awaiting him cheered. Nervously clutching his selected text, *Pete the Cat*, the teacher coordinator thought, "what if he has a hard time reading or doing this?" This student, all six feet of him, sat on a tiny chair made for a four-year-old. The teachers all shrugged, and he began to read. Suddenly the smile on his face seemed to broaden, and, as he finished the story, he high-fived and laughed with the little children. It was impossible not to be proud. This was his moment.

This child still runs a little too fast and talks a little too loud at times. Rather than boxing him into a corner and waving a finger while shouting a redirection at him, the teachers in this school now walk up pleasantly and change the subject or lower their tone: *when are you reading again? Are you doing good this week? I want to hear about you reading again.* This serves as a reminder to him that he is part of something bigger than himself and that this experience has a direct impact on the other psychological challenges he and children like him may face on an almost con-stant basis, turning to a positive more often.

A program like Middles to Littles may seem difficult to arrange. After all, most school principals do not inherit a pre-school, stumbling into an opportunity as the previously men-tioned school did. Yet schools moved to a virtual learning community for much of the 2020 school year when the world was faced with a raging pandemic. Video meetings are now commonplace as a byproduct of organizational transformations and virtually bringing programs like the one mentioned together is easier and may be the only viable option.

In fact, during the pandemic the same school who engineered Middles to Littles brought students together virtually. In an interesting twist, this was in many ways at least as beneficial and possibly more so because of the distress students faced while sitting out the physical school experiences of interacting in person with others amidst social isolation running rampant.

Therefore, like the transformation in this situation, use your school's newfound digital models to foster it if physical distance prevents in person visitations. Consider that every town has preschools that have popped up all over town, like a franchise restaurant chain, and there are in-district as well as private preschools everywhere. These preschools do not even have to be in your own town if done digitally, and you are in a small community. The point is, this can be replicated and after one school saw the powerful effects that "helpers high" had on some of its most troubled middle schoolers, it stands to reason your students most in need can benefit too.

There are alternatives to engage learners in with additional and quicker bursts to help them enjoy a "helpers high." One educator walked a student around the building, the child raging with anger and on the verge of exploding. The teacher began picking up trash that had blown up against the school on a typically chilly late-fall day while conversing with the student. After picking up the third piece of trash, the teacher observed his student pick up the next piece. He also picked up the one after that. This continued as the teacher thanked him for his help. This was not a request by the teacher.

The teacher did not even know if the student would follow along and thought instead of the act as a simple distraction tactic. Indeed, it was a distraction and this child's whole-body language and demeanor literally changed in just about a five-minute walk around the school, all while performing a good deed. This same child could be accused of drawing offensive graffiti in the bath-room. Quick techniques like this do not always work. But they often do, and it is worth trying for some improvement, rather than none.

## Curiosity Saves the Cat – A Quick Look at Treating Trauma

The differences between humans and cats are our evolved sense of self and where curiosity can serve to benefit us. There are good reasons why silly and binge-worthy video clips of cats run rampant online. Cats make us laugh because they often place themselves in precarious situations, at their own expense; born out of a curiosity that lands them in trouble, like hanging from a tree limb, or jumping at a squirrel on a TV screen.

Fortunately for humans, curiosity, while at times humorous, also helps us to evolve. That is precisely why evolution has engineered curiosity as a mechanism to place us in a state of mindfulness, a sense of deep thought, where insatiable human curiously is free to roam.

If curiosity is a tool, we can use to shift ourselves into a higher cognitive frame, could it work as a mechanism to address the destructive behaviors associated with anxiety, stress, and trauma? Famous entertainer Jewel thinks so and described, in her own experience, how she is living proof (Oaklander, 2020).

Before you write this off as unscientific anecdotal entertainer gibberish, consider the science behind how curiosity can orient us to a mindful, uniquely introspective temperament. Indeed, having an exploratory outlook that arouses curiosity, openness, and acceptance can set the stage for a cascade of higher-level problem solving, thinking and a reduction in anxiety, stress, and trauma. Counteract anxiety with curiosity, by teaching the learner to enlist their natural instincts, and thrust them into higher order thinking, away from distress.

Having established that curiosity is an uncomplicated and viable way to treat the effects of trauma, why then is this approach not enlisted more frequently? Perhaps we can find ways to invigorate the curiosity of our learners. Keep in mind that students under duress have a depressed and underdeveloped set of skills that literally inhibits their higher order cognitive exploration skills.

This is typically the result of primal instincts settling in. Changing this course even temporarily, with a curiosity mindset provides the circumstances for an experiential phenomenon that literally replaces the damage brought on by distress. Finding ways to get kids there as a productive substitute is well worth it.

Understandably, protective mechanisms serve us well under circumstances of clear and present danger. However, post-traumatic stress lingers on long after as the damaging residual effects of trauma and finding ways to engage children in their own curiosity requires more targeted methods. This starts with trust and skill, two characteristics of highly effective teachers.

Many of the techniques characterized in this book attest to strategies involving relationship building. Sustaining trust is the basis for effective teachers, who use their skill to provide an atmosphere for building and fostering relations. Using the techniques contained in this text as guidelines will garner a much more willing child participant. Cultivating this trust will take longer with children under duress and require greater patience. Yet it will come, using these techniques. Stacking them together will expand and hasten the response time for many students in need.

Teaching skill are naturally part of a highly effective teacher's repertoire. Yet the skill to build relations is something schools cannot rely blindly on, to hope for garnering student acceptance. Do not just count on natural teacher instincts to randomly spark students' curiosity. Cultivate it. The importance of professional development, and more specifically, how training is executed, must be prioritized. Methods for professional development to seize on best practices using targeted strategies are discussed in subsequent sections of this text.

Not surprisingly, some of the most effective professional development techniques are like those that engage learners in insatiable curiosity. These methods can drive higher, more functional cognitive processes. Consider providing dedicated professional development on best practices, and on a continuum, not simply once a year, or when you sense there is a need for it. These should be built into existing meeting frameworks and flexible learning approaches.

To provide a foundation for PD, use visionary planning and construct a regiment that fosters professional development, in anticipation of the need. This proactive methodology acknowledges once and for all that children need help, not after we are confronted with the surprise of their aberrant behavior, when it could be too late. In this unproductive scenario, adults are too often forced into reacting to an incident after an outburst.

Engaging children in their learning in ways that stimulate their interests and connects their learning to what matters to them is best mastered through thoughtful research. Invest in evidence-based practices and resources that can provide teachers with practical tools to engage their learners. Virtually all school districts are vested in making their teachers better at their trade, regardless of their differing and ranging community values, or political views, so we can aim for this set of best practices knowing they offer universally recognized goals.

Helping teachers to be better, by hiring better, and improving from within through professional development will certainly have the dual benefit of better instruction, and in engaging learners in their desired curiosity. Given the knowledge that curiosity helps the individual enter a mindful state, and that this fosters practical ways to address their challenges then appears to be a win-win in helping children grow and develop. They perform better while they are managing their own psychological profile; both of which are lifelong skills.

The key premise among these suggestions is again that they are not end-alls, and should not necessarily be imitated, or copied word for word. Rather, they are options, among a series of other choices and should be adapted to a school community's values and a child's unique needs. The point is that trauma can be tackled when you root children in programs that keep them away from discipline silos and focused on positive alternative interventions. They are replicable, adaptable, and best used stacked together. Working as standalones, the practitioner can see results too but these results are more limited.

## PD

Professional development must be research based and time tested; designed in ways that provide the foundation for how teachers are acclimated to help their students. Setting the conditions is important in the sequence for how educators can navigate targeted PD; the kind that is focused on implementing efficiently best practices. This is accomplished by providing recognition and support for the challenges teachers face; challenges which vary from school to school and from district to district.

Consider that traditional professional development (PD) models do not work as well as they have the capacity to. Applying the right approach helps move the bar. PD must be problem based, and tailored to educators' local needs, not by way of a broad-based and generalized set of ideals. Therefore, the PD must be adaptable, ready to be modified and transformed. This is one reason formats like Edcamps have gained in popularity.

Edcamps are grass-roots teacher-driven conferences, designed to offer current and relevant professional development for teachers. There flexibility appeals to the need for adaptability and strong association to current issues. Related to this is the concept of Pop-up PD, a method that one principal developed in response to needs showing up during Covid-19.

Pop-up PD is simple in practice. If there is a need that emerges, PD can be tailored specific to what is called for, whether it is a current challenge, or an emerging, long term one. Because of this, PD must allow for teacher input, as a framework for overall purpose to be sustained. Making the PD practical, relevant, and timely accentuates the purposeful application of it, and increases the willingness and engagement for recipients of the PD.

When educators are treated professionally, a facilitator's influence in helping them develop their application of practices increases. Planners of PD can design it with a meaningful purpose. For instance, if teachers can see the proof that instituting practices to address student trauma greatly improves their classroom management, they see tremendous value in the practice. This includes providing PD that enables teachers to be proactive actors, not passive recipients of the information.

Pop-up PD is something that gained a keen interest in the school where the principal incorporated it. Teachers were in immediate need of support and did not have the luxury of time to access it, during Covid-19 quarantine. The principal and instructional coach were receiving significant inquiries on how-to's for accessing digital technologies in the thrust of change that swept through their school, as happened in many across America and abroad.

The principal-coach team began offering short, 20-minute Pop-up PD voluntary sessions. This concept gained tremendous interest and was so attractive because it offered relevant guidance in short bursts that the faculty could use immediately. Like so many ideas that were born out of this crisis, the concept of short bursts of relevant and timely PD was carried out of the pandemic. It resulted in continued interest and success with supportive models to aid students in distress, to learn technologies, and spread ideas as opportunities amongst teachers.

Too often, we see educators pushed on an agenda due to outside forces that often dishearten or worse, drives them away. Instead, applying concepts like Popup PD and Edcamps to support children under duress works to influence teacher understanding by leveraging their very own professionalism. This is what makes these kinds of trainings so appealing.

Move teachers from a fixed "this is the way kids should be" mindset toward an open "this is what we're confronted with" perspective to apply fluidity in learning support. By understanding the *why* and then fostering a better understanding to establish more effective practices, we effectively shift teachers away from feeling pushed to effectively being persuaded to make the sensible choice.

## Chapter Summary

Utilize methods offered as a guide, not an exact prescription program and personnel support include:

I'm More Than Just That espouses the idea that individuals are more than just their problem, their background, their socioeconomic status, their gender orientation, or religious affiliation. This expands their potential, rather than limits it.

Mentorship has shown promising results and, if effectively implemented, can have profound effects on children in need. One school adopted a restorative approach, called RSP, which engaged school resource officers who were retired police officers with at-risk students. This helped to reverse the cycle of law enforcement and families who feel a lack of equity creates injustices. Additionally, teachers can serve as RSP mentors. Proper training and the right staff are the ingredients to success.

Middles to Littles engages at risk pre- and teen students with a sense of "helpers high," by reading to preschoolers. One school shows how this can be done, both in person and virtually, to promote a positive climate and engage challenging and distressed learners constructively.

Curiosity reverses the effects of trauma by engaging the individual in higher thought processes, in the executive functioning part of the brain, and engaging learners in their own insatiable curiosity to witness their angst melting away.

Professional Development – use PD as a way into training teachers to employ effective practices to help students move away from debilitating habits due to their trauma. Be adaptable to student needs in developing PD programming and allow for flexible opportunities for teachers to gain from PD. Edcamps and pop-up PD are examples of ways to flexibly manage PD to best address student trauma.

# 4

# Implementation and Training on Trauma – Preparation and PD

One of the greatest challenges and subsequent acknowledgements presented in this text is that practitioners, those in the trenches teaching and in contact with children everyday are not experts in treating stress disorders. They lack the training and professional knowledge to provide therapeutic approaches to children with trauma. Furthermore, they are not afforded the time to provide this level of intense support for children.

Therefore, they should never be burdened with this unreasonable expectation, alongside the rigorous challenges they face to meet the varied and complex demands already required of teachers. Fortunately, there are complementary methods teachers can participate in, which foster a support system, one which does not replace trained clinicians and counselors and instead, enables coordination as a boots-on-the-ground approach.

Liberating teachers from the role of trained clinician, we focus instead on benefits from the immediately impactful and efficient methods recommended within this text. These methods are not a panacea, and they should not be considered universal.

DOI: 10.4324/9781003162971-4

Rather, be mindful that stacking them provides the platform that just works for many kids, much of the time. Remember that we are not aiming to "cure" children, nor are these suggested as treatments. Call to mind that these practical methods are best implemented alongside trauma support and/or professional counseling.

Professional development and support for educators is not only a good idea, but it must also be considered indispensable. Simply dumping strategies or an article in the lap of the busy educator will not work. Worse, poor direction can result in regressions if approached incorrectly. Teachers should approach strategies like the good teaching practices they mastered in the classroom context.

Therefore, invest qualitative time during professional development to help build educators' understanding and then offer these practical techniques to be executed. The importance of helping educators break through their own fears over addressing childhood trauma cannot be understated.

Consider a survey of hundreds of teachers conducted by the American Federation of Teachers (2020). Eighty-five percent of respondents reported being uncomfortable with addressing students' anxiety, grief, and trauma resulting from Covid-19. Among a faculty of 50 teachers then, only seven or eight would feel equipped to support children in distress from the pandemic. That is an alarming figure when you consider the contrast that veteran teachers are far more likely to report comfort delivering content and managing student conduct.

Certainly Covid-19 has been a massive case study in trauma, and we can learn from it to support children. Yet there will be other traumas, both macro, like the pandemic, and micro, like the unexpected death of a family member. If the survey previously mentioned is any indication of how faculty members feel about their own qualifications to address the rising crisis of trauma in large scale and more personal matters, school communities would be wise to adopt approaches showing teachers that they can and will be equipped to support and help children grow on the other side of trauma.

The good news is that schools can institute supports which bring confidence and comfort to teachers working to aid children impacted by trauma. The concepts presented in this text lay the groundwork for a data-based approach that refers to science and anecdotal evidence, situating the practitioner with the resources and training necessary to help. Start by structuring your PD Program to meet the needs outlined.

## Framing Your PD Program

Educational leaders and professional development planners should be prepared to design a plan for faculty; one that considers the circumstances of the given community needs. Concrete options are presented, that are connected to the descriptions outlined in Chapter 3 and provided in greater depth. Collecting information, using this information, and individualizing it are all considerations in design as they are tailored to meet the needs of students in need.

### Examples of Practices to Institute

Following are methods offered as an inventory to draw from. These are designed to be replicable and are inexpensive; the two ingredients necessary for any successful program that will sustain with success.

## Survey Your Faculty About Their Concerns

Influencing faculty through surveying offers them a choice, and options empower them, lubricating the parts of your machine that need to keep forging ahead. By steering faculty toward a common framework of concerns and goals, and establishing options for how to address them, teachers can gain ownership and help move the goal forward.

This was discovered in a school where faculty meetings were transformed into authentic experiences that allowed the professionals to gain selection power and liberated them to participate in hands on, proactive approaches to address issues. Previously, the faculty dreaded their 3:00 pm monthly meetings, seated in the auditorium, and exhausted after a long day. They paid little attention to the administrative agenda, and that was the problem: it was the administrative agenda, not within their control.

Promoting choice through survey invigorates a faculty and empowers your team to take ownership. Faculty members want the best interests of students served, and either agree in principle with the overall goals of the school to achieve this or may offer even more creativity in uncovering ways to achieve it. This happens when you get professionals working together, developing, and creating innovative solutions. It is the multiplier effect; the ability by your team to be additive in their ideas exponentially generating better ones.

The multiplier effect compounds the thought energy of groups, collecting information that operates on higher levels to attribute to a magnified effect. The common phrase, "two heads are better than one," speaks to this. Arranging this in a structured format engages professionals in ways that increase their resourcefulness beyond the numerical value proportional to the group.

### *Measure Outcomes*

Google borrowed an idea from a company named 3M that allowed their employees to have one day a week to work on a project that was of personal interest to them, in their professional pursuits. That 20% time remarkably netted up to 80% productivity, including the invention of Gmail. The real payoff is contained within the framework's flexibility. Like Google employees, when faculty have choice in how they address an issue, and commit to a plan, remarkably positive solutions result.

Offering faculty workable models that they can learn about today, and use tomorrow is one of the most pivotal points in this text. If your faculty and you take nothing else away from this text, at least they can start using these tools that are suggested, immediately. That is the point of educators not trained in therapy: getting many of their students on track, most of the time. That is progress, not perfection.

When faculty master something that is replicable and this practice is possible without harrowing and long-term approval processes or tight fiscal budgets, buy in and momentum increase substantially. Faculty engage in ways that help them institute ideas sooner, and with greater results. Seeing agents of change in the lives of children without filibusters gets teachers on board, championing the collective cause. Enlisting faculty surveys and using this feedback helps spark a kind of collective soul and focus.

Professional learning communities are operational and because faculty take ownership, they truly benefit from a tangible and relevant opportunity that matters more intimately to them. Since professional development is such an important component of preparation for the success of faculty identifying and learning how to manage in-class moments with children exhibiting signs of trauma, continue to engage faculty in innovative methods to learn about them. Edcamps were discussed previously and serve as a model for this perspective. They will be detailed at greater length here.

## Edcamps – The Un-Faculty Meeting!

Edcamp is an engaging way to inspire teachers to learn best practices from colleagues. While they are popular, buzzing events, these often take place outside of the school day, on a Saturday, or require a teacher to leave their classroom duties to participate.

This can be an impediment to getting faculty on board. Not only does this take faculty away from their duties or personal and family interests, but those who attend Edcamp-style events are already motivated to extend their professional learning.

Consider engaging everyone, including those with busy lives outside of school, and the lesser convinced. You will begin to see real changes take place in your school.

True progress is made when we engage faculty that sit between the unwilling, and the motivated members on your team. The majority of faculty represent this group and tipping them your way will help to address challenges in a more substantial manner, getting most (not all) on board. We always aspire to influence and persuade our faculty, not to make them comply, which has the reverse effect, causing resistance.

An important note about getting most of your staff on board: if you wait for everyone to buy-in and be on board, with any new effort or PD concept, you will never get there. Focus on the majority, and quite frankly, ignore the minority who resist. Otherwise, too much energy is wasted.

Whatever age group you are working with, you can expect to encounter at least one negative nelly, and you already know who they are. While you do not want to give this person a platform by challenging him or her, you are best suited at moving the masses. That is where change happens. You will recognize the shift, like a tide rolling onto the beach.

So how do we begin? Construct your PD in ways that are built into an existing framework of your school schedule. This can be pre-scheduled team meetings, faculty meetings, or dedicated professional development days. Often, these days are mistakenly handed over to costly outside specialists or worse, feel like busywork for faculty. That is not effective. Instead, assemble an Edcamp-style PD format to engage your faculty in real training opportunities that encourage them, within your pre-existing structures.

Consider an approach that sets the stage for vibrant learning. Having created a foundation for PLC platforms, allow teachers discretion, within a general framework and focus on supporting children with challenges, difficult children, and those who exhibit signs of trauma. An Edcamp is participant driven and feels like the spirited energy of a conference. This fosters momentum-friendly aesthetic surroundings, so the stage is set.

Edcamps work well because they are designed around community participation and coordination. They are genuine ways to attract faculty with the motivation and learning that happens at a grassroots level. Programmatically, Edcamps are highly choice driven by faculty. Offering a menu of ideas and allowing the participants to take much more responsibility in how the event is fostered promotes responsibility and willingness. This is not someone else's idea. It becomes theirs!

Here is how to implement this highly engaging "un-conference:"

1. Designate an organizer. This can be anyone with respected influence in your school. Therefore, administrators do not have to manage the event. In fact, it is a good idea that they do not, if you want to encourage buy in, especially from *fence-sitters*. Enlist an informal leader, or coach.

2. Develop topic ideas. These are organized around a theme. Let the faculty run with it. Remember, use survey to spark ideas. Then create a menu of choices focused on this list generated by direct feedback. One way to do this is to initiate two, 25-minute mini sessions in a one-hour meeting. Lengthier meetings can allow for additional breakouts.

3. Develop a registration process. Use a simple form for registrants to sign up and arrange meeting rooms for the sessions near each other. Faculty will have the energy of a conference feel for checking in and out of sessions.

4. Confirm sign ups to attendees and make clear where and when they will attend. You can do this by pulling data from the sheet that the form feeds into. Mail merge tools are a way to effectively manage this in a more personalized context for teachers.

5. Encourage the context for experimentation that helps faculty innovate together. This is a bonding experience that perpetuates, resulting from the multiplier effect. Let them

be creative and solution oriented. This rejuvenates them and enhances their energy.

6. Always consider this along a continuum. One and done conferences and workshops are only effective in the short term. Consider phases of future Edcamp sessions, tied to the earlier ones, so that they are all interconnected and make visionary sense in your overall progress and work together.

Make this feel truly like a conference. You can accomplish this by issuing certificates of completion – a personalized touch. Have coffee and inexpensive pens out for giveaways. See the section on donations or buy these cheap to manage cost. Additionally, follow up with more survey feedback. What worked, what can be improved or adjusted, what would you like to see in a future session? Always follow up with relevant and responsive PD. Faculty will see and appreciate the plausible connection to become more connected and collaborative.

Do faculty really think Edcamps are that great? Here is what was reported in research by Carpenter and Linton (2018, pp. 60–65):

Over nine out of ten respondents reported Edcamps *altered* their practices. Instructional practice was one of two reported shifts faculty made following the Edcamp. Participants acknowledged obstacles to and supported acting on what they had learned from. Therefore, building in a framework to allow for professional development, and the follow up continuum are vital to the best application of Edcamp training.

Of tremendous substance, learner impact resulted in improved engagement, experiences, and dispositions (Carpenter & Linton, 2018, pp. 65–66). This fact alone makes it well worth instituting Edcamp training, for the benefit of professional development. By providing educators with a level of training that directly administers to them the tools to enhance student growth in engagement, curiosity gets a boost, and benefits of curiosity were discussed earlier.

Likewise, enhanced experience and disposition on learning are both elevated in ways that improve a student's outlook. Strong support for instituting Edcamps in place of PD or faculty meetings is clear. Yet recent conditions made the vibrant aesthetics of an Edcamp seemingly impossible. After all, educators spent nearly a year watching moderately engaging webinars, sitting glued to our computers, encountering the harsh effects of "Zoom gloom," resulting from Covid-19.

That is because being onscreen is a more tiring experience then being in person; it requires participants to attend with much more effort to process and make sense of body language, and vocal cues like pitch and tone. When in person, these cues are much less demanding to follow. Our brains are more qualified to interpret three-dimensional in person experiences over these more challenging two-dimensional digital experiences.

The pandemic caused a transformation in teaching and learning due to these obstacles. Sometimes, online access is a better avenue for mobility and economy. So how do we get the live benefits of Edcamps in a video conference call? One school accomplished this in an inventive way that made those who experienced it decide to continue with the setup, when in person experiences became an option again. It required planning and coordination just as in-person Edcamps do; an approach that resulted from the lessons learned in digital learning during 2020. Here are the steps to make digital Edcamps work:

Step 1:
The facilitator sets up the event, by developing a theme, gaining feedback from an interest survey of responses by participants. Develop these into a choice menu. This part is just like the in-person Edcamp planning.
Step 2:
Have volunteers who are willing to share their ideas be organized around a theme by spending a quick 2–3 minutes providing an overview, on the video conference. This

phase is very much like a webinar, except that there is a choice to select from the handful of topics where presenters create the environment that is more like an in person Edcamp.

Step 3: Connect participants to the event and let them choose digital rooms to visit.

    a) Since participants cannot visit the physical classrooms where presenters are sharing, bring the classroom to them. Breakout rooms enable the facilitator to set up the event, and then allow participants to pick where they will go (*"Self-select Breakout Rooms in Zoom | Allow participants to choose breakout room,"* 2020, 03:15–05:21) for a deeper Q&A experience.

    b) Just like the grassroots in-person Edcamp, participants can stay as long as they wish, and depart when they decide to visit another room. This is not out of order; it is encouraged!

Step 4:

Edcamps are participant driven, so some ideas are preselected by teachers. Yet what makes the Edcamp experience so unique, is the in the moment creation of new sessions, born of the creative and collaborative element participants immerse themselves in. If you are willing to get even more innovative, allow individuals to offer this pop-up flexibility, in fact promote and encourage it!

Step 5:

Recall that professional development needs to be adaptive, improved, and adjusted to continue to evolve for the needs of the recipients. Be prepared to survey your faculty about what they liked, what they disliked, accept recommendations, and make course corrections. Do not view the feedback of constructive criticism as anything more than ways to improve the experience. This is already an improvement over traditional PD and your faculty are now eager to take the experience a step further!

As previously discussed, one of the biggest benefactors of highly invigorating Edcamp experiences are students. First, students benefit from teachers who are better informed about innovative topics. Teachers report that they are likely to be better at their practice due to an Edcamp experience. Engagement is also reported to increase by learners, due to teachers altering their teaching practices to be more progressive as learned in the Edcamp (Carpenter & Linton, 2018, p. 65).

Second, many teachers who experienced a digital version of an Edcamp were so enthusiastic that they decided to run their own Edcamp event, for students in their classroom. This is digitally viable. The facilitator can access breakout rooms to oversee with greater ease than in-person, where spreading unsupervised children out across physical spaces is more difficult. Students are also digital natives, capable of acting more quickly after some basic instruction. Imagine their excitement as they embark on their own Edcamp!

Finally, a call for educators to volunteer to participate is noble, a contribution larger than themselves, and teachers profess great satisfaction in doing so. As one experienced administrator noted, truly original ideas, from all corners of the school emerged. The tragedy is letting those ideas die in that corner, left unshared with so many others, at the sacrifice of students who could have, and should have benefited from them. That is what Edcamps are all about; idea sharing to enrich the education of all learners.

## Story to Link Meaning and Understanding

Throughout this text, story is weaved into concepts to illustrate a point, and story is discussed in different ways as methods for aiding children and their teachers. There is no coincidence that the use of story plays such a considerable role as a strategy for helping individuals heal. Applying the tools of story has a profound impact on how we can help children and educators.

Presentation of content can be administered more effectively when delivered by a storyline, rather than disseminated as information that is strictly factual. Stories connect us to one another and help us identify with characters within a narrative. Consider the receptivity that occurs when someone identifies with circumstances in a story. It is not uncommon to hear an individual profess, *I am like that*, or *I have done that*. Story creates safety, a security for the recipient that allows them to acknowledge and identify, rather than deny.

Alternatively, if someone encounters blunt criticism, it is human nature for one to put up their primal defenses, operating within the archaic, less evolved hindbrain and medulla of our brain. We feel like cavemen and women, fighting for survival. This has the effect of impeding our ability to see the parts of that criticism that help us advance. Primal instincts are protective, and while they are rarely needed in today's world, can overrun our sense of better judgment, so we do not see how to reason out our understanding, and more importantly, how feedback can help us.

When a well-orchestrated story presents a criticism to the recipient, our higher order functions are activated. This affects problem solving, impulse control and objective reasoning. Someone who is highly reflective and non-defensive, is operating within this more advanced area of neural functioning. In this realm, we are quite simply calibrated to be more receptive. That is where the use of story fits in.

Something extraordinary happens when information is delivered by a story rather than by a deliberation of facts, or statements: more of our brain switches on. When we hear a story, the neural activity increases by five times (VanDeBrake, 2018), like a switchboard that has instantly lit up the map of our mind.

Putting our mindset in this higher state of mind facilitates a more accepting, open willingness. Consider Ted Talks, 18-minute, story-lined lessons with relevant messages. Ted Talks are designed to get an important idea across through story, and to do so in the optimal frame of time known for peak attention – less than 20 minutes. Storytellers can influence our mindset in positive, and alternatively in negative ways.

Negative messaging is mentioned as a caution regarding the falsehoods and misinformation presented in social media. Negative social media and the storylines fictionalized or grossly exaggerated bear a heavy cost on our thinking and in fact, a powerful impact in negatively tapping our primal senses. Absent inspiring or motivational stories, negative and false ones should almost always be avoided, unless real and present danger is accurately portrayed, and that can be found within more trusted sources.

Using story in a beneficial way enables us to convey a message to our faculty that reinforces the importance of their work, and to do so in a manner that opens the door to a willingness to learn and help students in crisis. Story has the added benefit of maintaining greater retention than strictly factual delivery. Weaving important information throughout stories is a viable path to get the necessary information across, and to do so far more persuasively.

Some stories get the door open, like the Blueberry Story (Vollmer, 2011). This is an inspiring anecdote about a businessman who learned that lecturing teachers about producing the perfect student (like the perfect blueberry) was a lost cause. He was himself transformed by the challenges' teachers faced, and how to help them overcome these obstacles. Conveying through story is important for opening closed minds, and they are worth the time to incorporate, rather than spending hours trying to convince someone by presenting dry facts.

Other stories can teach us how to institute best practices. Some remain timeless, and include *Three Letters from Teddy* (Ballard, 1974), a story of triumph for a young struggling student after a teacher decided to put aside her preconceived notions. What is so compelling about this story is that it allows teachers the safety to acknowledge that there are some kids they just do not like. This is often an unspoken (sometimes not!) truth that by acknowledging, we can move past biases and begin to genuinely help children, especially those with more challenges that we encounter.

Consider that the reasons teachers do not like some children are varied and complex. Yet one chief premise that this story operates from is that we may not have the whole story. Incorporated into this narrative are ways in which the teacher constructed relationship building opportunities that helped her accept and commit to a path toward reaching the child in more substantive ways. That is progress.

Undoubtedly there are other stories with different information that should be conveyed to teachers, which empower them to use this information to help children. Using story opens the door to our willingness that is rare to find when presenting a PowerPoint with facts, or sending a memo citing district goals. Instead, illustrating your point with a story has lasting effects that will aid the teacher in gaining better understanding. This enables them to reflect more constructively, more critically about how and why we must strive to help our traumatized learners.

## MicroPD

Like much that has been shared in this text, time is limited and expensive. We cannot afford to mismanage it to get the best quality in the shortest amount of time. Teachers are still teachers and they must deliver content, assess students, communicate with parents and families, reteach where gaps exist, and more. Mismanaging teacher time is not only an annoyance to professionals, but also downright costly.

Most schools have structures where teachers and school counselors meet weekly to discuss grade level, team, or department progress of shared students. Tasked with helping students achieve and dealing with the diverse challenges of students and parents, they can become energy depleted. Setbacks can aggravate regression; not seeing growth is discouraging and can make educators struggle, feeling exasperated.

At the beginning of the year, when everyone is energized and well-rested, looking forward to helping all children, school teams set out to achieve well intended goals. As the year drags on, and educators are looking over their shoulder at the high-pressure stakes of preparing students for standardized testing, managing behavior issues and more, these visionary goals can take a back seat. Throughout the year, it is important to inject energy when it is needed most, and helping students gain from this can be accomplished in short bursts, through something called MicroPD (Gaskell, 2020, pp. 80–81).

To help teachers transform from a professional development (PD) experience, supports must go deeper than the one-and-done workshop. To do PD right, there must be more sustained, relevant, and tangible takeaways. Recurring PD sessions are informative and elicit teacher input. The impact of short bursts of rejuvenating practices depends on the premise of mini sessions, or MicroPD. Design five- to eight-minute invigorating opportunities for teachers to benefit from a practice that helps them bond. Think of this as an infusion that helps teachers through the hard parts.

Here is how MicroPD works:

1. Introduce the concept: "Today, we're going to try something reenergizing, since it's mid-year and we're all struggling with persistent student issues and misconduct."
2. Read a team-building quote and have teachers reflect on it for 30 seconds to 1 minute. Example: *We're all different but as a team we fit together.*
3. Next, ask each team member to share how the quote applies to his or her team.
4. Last, the facilitator shares her own contribution.

Teachers report enjoying this experience, as it revitalizes them, empowering each through a bonding experience. They jump right into the rest of the meeting with willingness, energy, humor, and creativity. Optimal energy and focus are what make teams creative. This is necessary when managing complicated and layered student issues like trauma. This simple, easy-to-replicate concept can occur regularly, and a facilitator can inject some fun ideas into the activity, such as having a teacher offer their own unique trivia or other inspiring concepts.

The team can close the meeting with something interesting and/or positive that was experienced. This reinforces the bonding experience, critical for teamwork, collaboration, and creativity that is necessary to help distressed learners. Educators are not so distant and disconnected from when they are able to learn something distinctive about each other.

MicroPD has the advantage of being quick, and re-energizing, bonding faculty together, right before they go back into their classrooms and teach their students. What better way to set the stage with a positive outlook on the children who are in most need of it? There is nothing more compelling than teachers sharing with their colleagues. It is at the foundation of every successful team and students benefit from refreshed, positive teachers.

## The Stories That Teach Us How to Teach Them

Late one morning, the principal sat in a meeting with his teachers, a professional learning community like so many before. But there would be something different about this one. Unlike other meetings, he had not risked this idea, because for so long, he could not talk about it. Serving as the school leader, credibility had to be protected. It was not something you would add to your resume and point to and say, "look, I am an expert in this area." Or was it?

The purpose of this meeting was to help teachers understand that children with challenges are so much more than their challenges, and that when it seems most difficult to do so, they should dig deeper to recognize this, to never give up on any one of them. He had tried many other ways and it was a time of year when the honeymoon period of September, new clothes and the fresh smell of fall leaves were long gone. This was the dead of winter, with months of school remaining, and frowns on teachers faces at the challenges presented to them by difficult students, and students in difficult situations.

Teachers were tired, especially with those few students who drained their energy the most. *Why should we bother with that kid? It's obvious that they don't want my help*, or *They are too far behind to catch up, or their parents won't follow up* . . . The refrain was all too common and while there was merit to their frustration, the cost was too high and the opportunity too great to roll over in agreement.

The term "opportunity" may strike the reader as being in direct contrast to the evidence. We all know *that kid* or *those kids*. We have seen the challenges, and the frustrations when enduring the constant barrage of confrontation and let downs. Convinced the principal had talked about others to try to persuade teachers to look past their deficits long enough, it was worth the risk, at this point to try an activity he had thought about doing for years but was too afraid to dare.

He carefully laid out the documents, one after another illustrating details about a child who was clearly beyond hope, doomed to failure, just like so many others that these teachers had become familiar with. They were reminded of a child who dropped out, or ended up in prison, or struggled with addiction later in life, chillingly confirming their biases.

The child's identity was carefully concealed, although not for the reason the teachers suspected (confidentiality). Here were some of the conclusions that were drawn about the student by a child study team who had run a battery of tests on the student when signs of risk were clear:

- ◆ Ability in the below average, slow learner intelligence range.
- ◆ Depressed verbal scores.

- Significantly depressed on social awareness and interactions.
- Academic achievement six months below grade level.
- Shows hostility and poor impulse control.
- Self-expectations appear unrealistically high – talks about college and a career as a doctor.

Grades were consistently low. Detentions, a suspension, and more blanketed the student's file. This child was noticeably at risk, and most definitely headed for predictable failure. The principal asked the teachers after reviewing, analyzing, and discussing these documents what recommendations they might make, followed by what predictions they inferred.

*He Should Be Classified. He Should Receive Intervention and Referral Services. He Must Have Come From an Urban School. He Needs Better Parenting.*

Next, they postulated his future. Their forecast? *He will drop out, get arrested, repeat a grade, struggle with addiction . . .*

Now was the big reveal. He shared that they all knew this child. They had worked with him. Puzzled, they inquired with nervous urgency, "But I thought this was confidential?" "No," the principal persisted, "you know this child." "Who?!?" One of the teachers finally blurted out, "was it you?!'" A timely pause and then he announced, "Yes, you are looking at him."

He recalls feeling a bit nervous for a moment, wondering if he had lost all credibility with this highly respected group of teachers. Then after a pause, another said, "Dr. G, are you kidding?"

To say that they were surprised would have been an understatement. He had let the cat out of the bag. The child with such a poor prognosis was . . . him. You could see on their faces a sense of puzzled intrigue and shock. How had he ended up here? How had he far exceeded the expectations of those reports? Remember, his expectations for self were "unrealistically high," but . . . he did not know that. He would often reflect that not knowing this was in fact some part of his accidental fortune.

This administrator was once a kid, struggling to navigate obvious learning and behavioral challenges. Yet somewhere, someway, and somehow, important people came along and did not give up on his younger self. Considerations can be explored for how some of his accidental fortunes could be crafted with intention into ways to increase the likelihood that children like him, facing obstacles could and should be encouraged to overcome and go beyond their limitations.

The principal used this (and continues to) as a reference point for his teachers to understand the important lesson from that day. Numerous teachers in that meeting came to see him later privately, too embarrassed to admit that they had been a prisoner to their own biases in telegraphing a child's future prematurely and unfairly. They committed with a promise to never do that again.

The risk this principal took was well worth the lesson about framing perspective for all children and how any child, any underdog has the capacity to achieve far beyond their expectations, *if* the adults around them refuse their inclination and believe. That is transformational growth through professional development. This activity serves as an excellent reference point for helping reinforce for teachers the possibilities within any child, including those that are most effected by trauma.

## Replication

As educators, we may feel as though we do not have a story as profound to share as this one. Yet every one of us has encountered some struggle in our own unique way and did not fail because we refused to give up, whether in academics, athletics, or other pursuits. Dig deep and be courageous in sharing your own story with colleagues, and your students, to show that they too can survive, and even thrive. Students gain greater trust and support for educators, willing to open up and connect through understanding and empathy that is derived from a transparent account of their own true struggles.

## The Pygmalion Effect

Examples of subconscious bias like this story are well illustrated and date back to a groundbreaking study in 1963, conducted by Robert Rosenthal and Lenore Jacobson, at an elementary school in San Francisco, California (University of Wisconsin – Madison Psychology Department, n.d.).

In this experiment, some teachers were told that they were teaching above-average students, and others were told they were teaching below-average students. The teachers in the *above-average* group had higher expectations for their students, who subsequently performed above expectations. The *below-average* students (who were in fact the same level performers as the "high" group) performed below their actual proficiency level.

Rosenthal and Jacobson concluded that the teacher's preconceptions of their student's ability to achieve influenced the student's actual performance. This study offered profound findings and yet, more than a half century later, there remains a persistent lack of consciousness for the inequities based on preconceived notions in our society. Using resources like this text, educators should seize on this opportunity to break down the barriers that were systematized for too long, use science and good practice to alter outcomes for all learners, particularly for those facing the most distress, and start the path to institutionalizing equity over bias.

## Chapter Summary

PD is necessary, more now than ever, as the recognition of trauma is evident, and recent events like Covid-19 that harbored students in their homes away from school access points, and equity concerns have increased the distress students encounter.

Recent evidence of more effective PD demonstrates access points that teachers and schools should embrace to better equip them with skill sets to support children. Begin your journey with feedback from your teachers. Surveying them reinforces your interest in their concerns, regarding a larger theme and responding to the survey gets them connected in empowering ways. Engaging teachers in this collaborative format enhances the benefits of multiple individuals working together. Allowing for some creativity generates inventive thinking in faculty at the grass roots level.

Edcamps can be fostered, both in person and digitally, now that there is evidence both works, and work extremely well in helping to support children under duress.

A powerful way to help teachers connect to kids in need is using narrative and storytelling. While this is generally limited to use in clinical settings, it is beneficial for teachers, who are natural story tellers to engage in.

MicroPD is a mini-PD method that is quick, effective and offers teachers the opportunity to bond in ways that benefit their students in greatest need. It is best to employ when teachers are facing their own distress, to reverse engineer their output to children.

Using personal challenges and sharing these as ways to teach the teachers, who will then teach their students is a bold and courageous way to get children on board, to see the light beyond their own challenges.

A half a century ago, an experiment proved that teacher expectation of students raises, or lowers, student performance. Leveraging this understanding to reverse students debilitating ways of performing helps them turn it all around.

# 5

# Actionable Ideas to Institute Right Now

## Provide Tangible Examples

It is important to underscore that there is no panacea, no original inventions offered via this field guide for helping children through crisis. Rather, unlike brand new and unproven concepts, what is unique is that these are compiled into a neatly organized methodology, with the stacking mechanisms characterized previously. Accompanying this is the encouragement for use of techniques with far greater patience and adaptability.

Therefore, some ideas are adapted, others borrowed from other fields, particularly to refocus on student and child trauma supports. Many of the evidence-based concepts offered are practical solutions for adults, organizations, and other self-improvement ideologies. Yet they are absent or grossly underrepresented in representing these techniques to support children. They are missing from field-based, day-to-day school life to support traumatized children. Or they are focused on clinical settings. Following are an accounting of practical, tangible methods to support children in distress.

DOI: 10.4324/9781003162971-5

## The Two-Minute Intervention

There are various renditions of quick interventions ( Minahan, 2019; McKibben, 2014; *How to: Use the Power of Personal Connection to Motivate Students: 4 Strategies*, n.d.), all with similar premises. The fundamentals of this version are that a teacher takes just two minutes a day, for an extended period, typically ten days (two weeks) to engage selected children in objective, safe, targeted, and supportive informal dialogue.

The two-minute intervention may sound simplistic. Be mindful that it must be sustained, and the teacher must remain objective. Adding perceived bias will reduce the qualitative value of delivery. Children, especially those who are traumatized are already highly protective and keen to shield from attempts that are less than authentic. Electronic or hard copy resources like the one in Appendix C are helpful to both structure and maintain logging, to sustain and monitor this technique.

Like many of the techniques proposed, this method may seem counterintuitive. Two-minute interventions are generally explored as a strategy when dealing with disruptive students. Why, a practitioner might ask, would we give attention to a child who is typically seeking negative attention? Anyway, wouldn't this backfire?

Notice that the word attention ends the inquiry, as in *negative attention*. One can replace negative with other words, and still observe that the underlying *desire* by the child is to seek *attention*, to be noticed. Flipping the option in a positive direction, to constructive feedback is something difficult, and often, traumatized children are not accustomed to it.

That is why it takes time and strategy. Ten days is no guesstimate. It is the point of a sustained, targeted, and tracked sequence. Unlearning behavior is far more difficult than learning behavior. Think about your own personal struggles when breaking a bad habit. We almost unconsciously forget about the learning process but must bring back to the conscious mind a practice that forces the habit out, through sustained effort.

Two-minute interventions are ideal for classroom environments where student conferencing is integrated as a pre-existing framework within the teacher's regular instruction. Allowing for a conferencing table and as a natural component of the teacher's instruction provides for the viability of this structure to be instituted. Sustain this with targeted patience and you can turn the tide.

## The One-Sentence Intervention

The premise of the one-sentence intervention is very much like the two-minute intervention. Yet as you can see, it is far more concise. One sentence is not a two-minute conversation; it may take seconds. This option while similar is presented because some children may remain averse to a lengthier dialogue (even of just two minutes), or the practitioner may have less time to practically institute a longer intervention.

Keeping the communication succinct may offer for children who find more extended (yes even just two minutes) dialogue more difficult, even exhaustive. Many traumatized children are inclined to prefer abridged communication and keeping the sentence objectively positive is likewise an instrument in the toolkit of the practitioner to consider. See Appendix D for a step-by-step guide for applying this practice.

The aim is to share two to three neutral statements over a period of a week to two weeks. These are objective in nature (absent your opinion), such as, *I heard that you play video games during your free time.* After establishing this over a period of five to ten days, move next to positive statements, such as, *I noticed that when you listen to music, you are more focused and work well.*

The shift from neutral to positive wording occurs when you can surmise that the timing is right. The student is more readily able to accept your positive statements as trustworthy, built on the previous objective statements. Start small, and subtle, and build off of these.

Issue the positive statements over a period of a week, or two; be cautious as traumatized students will be on guard about why you are complimenting them. This is also why it is important to be brief, succinctly characterizing the positive observation. You may even want to alternate days you issue positives for a while, until the student becomes more acquainted with your positive statements, and more comfortable hearing you state them. Observe the behavior and response change.

The one sentence intervention offers multiple benefits. First, it is reasonable to accept that busy educators may not have two or more minutes daily to target students with positive affirmations, encouragement, and support (although this is another problem, addressed in another section of the book). Thus, the one-sentence intervention becomes much more sustainable since it is a fraction of seconds. A ten-second affirmation that can have some or almost as much impact as a lengthier one clearly offers considerable value and does so efficiently.

Second, the one-sentence intervention is more easily replicable. It involves a quicker cycle to master the simpler concept and can more seamlessly unfold in the context of the dozens of interactions that occur in a typical classroom. Additionally, and perhaps most profoundly, techniques like the one-sentence intervention are likely to be more quickly and effectively transferable to students. This offers a window for their readiness to invoke skills of their own independently.

Transfer of the strategy should always remain the end goal, since ultimately, the student cannot take the teacher along with them everywhere following the initial intervention. This is true for virtually all interventions discussed in this text, yet especially ones like the one-sentence intervention. Its simplicity coincides with the known evidence that this uncomplicated, yet effective strategy is one more option to teach, and transfer to children.

Bear in mind other methods have value and should be introduced where possible. Yet, we should consider who and with what methods they will most benefit. Teaching children any of these skills offers tremendous, effective, short- and long-term support. That is why we must strive to pass on the strategy to learners. We want to minimize the possibility that children regress to an earlier stage of the post traumatic growth process, short of maintaining positive strategies.

To accomplish this, begin by providing students with brief, powerful words of encouragement and as children show responsiveness, after a sustained period of commitment to delivering the message daily, prepare to hand off, rather than exit from and abandoning a strategy, as a transformative opportunity for the learner.

On the other hand, like any other technique presented in this text, do not push this to the brink of a negative response point, or when a child is not ready. If after a sustained period, the student has shown little or even a regressive reaction, it may be best to abandon the approach, and move on to another method.

Often, students are not receptive to more assertive techniques until later. This is analogous to parents raising children and wondering if their kids will ever listen to them, only to realize that their children were listening all along. They just needed the skill of readiness to accept and practice the idea.

Assuming students demonstrate readiness, consider resources like the *Power of The One-Sentence Journal* (Newman, 2015), or variations of this concept. These are easy to follow, and can be embedded across content areas, even into a literacy program, health class, social studies, or other content area. Like most effective in-school interventions, those that succeed in class integrate into a pre-existing delivery by the teacher.

Keep in mind that learners who struggle with literacy may not benefit from writing interventions. This could have the opposite effect we desire, causing the child even greater anxiety. In these instances, use online resources to dictate a sentence. This engages students who struggle with transferring their thoughts to paper by verbalizing them.

Web-based programs like Speech Notes (Speech Notes, n.d.) are simple enough to operate on almost any device. Simply paste the narrated text dictated by the student into a document. A bank of positive affirmations can be offered as a menu to select from. These are plentiful online, try one, like at Pathways 2 Success (Pathway 2 Success, n.d.).

There are many other tools that are student-friendly which can be modelled for use by teachers and handed over to students. More will be discussed about self-talk, journaling and transferring post traumatic growth techniques from teacher to student in the goal setting section of this text.

## Praise and Getting the Ratio Right

John Gottman shared research results about married couples, in which the concept was straightforward. Praise your partner five times more than you criticize them and expect lifelong marriage success and happiness (Benson, 2017). His work has been borrowed by positive behavior support programs, instituted in schools, and translated into classroom use. Yet little is apparent in the literature about this simple and effective technique to implement, particularly for traumatized children.

It would seem straightforward: like married couples, implement a system where the teacher praises kids more frequently than they criticize, keeping the positive reinforcement ratio higher than negative statements, and tracking this to ensure the numbers are committed to. This is a method, well worth employing while being aware of the authenticity that must go along with carrying it out. That is because praise must be believable, and praise occurs less often for children suffering from trauma. This needs to be reversed.

One special education teacher recalled saying hello to a child who clearly exhibited signs of trauma, on 99 consecutive days. His warm greeting daily, with a genuine smile was patient, direct and sincere. For each of those 99 days, the student ignored him, and slumped into his chair for the day. The student was accustomed to adults giving up on him. This adult did not. Something happened one day in February. On the one hundredth day, that student turned to him and responded warmly, "hello!"

Unfortunately, many traumatized children have experienced the all too frequent sense that adults give up on them, letting them down. This may be a chicken and egg scenario. Consider: is it true that adults ultimately give up on these children, or is it that the child is so committed to the expectation that they set up the cause for this to happen? Does it matter? At this point, it is either happening, or being perceived to be happening, and that is where kids lose.

Know that with many of our traumatized learners, breaking that hard outer shell will be more complicated and challenging. Teachers must consider not just the quantity of the delivery, but the quality of their message. Indeed, the authenticity of your communication carries more weight than what you are often saying.

If a teacher is presenting a child with a canned comment of praise, she will quickly pick up on this. Look for genuine opportunities to praise a child. If it helps, have a list of common positives prepared, relevant to the context, no matter how small or subtle the positive is that you observe. Having this list in mind frames your thinking and prepares you to issue the praise when the timing is right. It takes some practice but with time and effort, works.

Bear in mind that being authentic specifically with praise and generally in communication means that 100% of messaging to learners does not need to be exclusively positive. In fact, this flies in the face of authenticity. No one is perfect, always, and children know this well.

Never issuing negative reinforcement or constructive criticism ignores this reality, making the praise when it is issued less believable. This defeats the purpose of building rapport and helping students gain a sense of confidence about their true large and small accomplishments.

Consider that there is an upper limit to the amount of positive feedback we deliver with effectiveness. Exceeding a ratio of 12 positive expressions to 1 negative can be seen as causing an adverse effect, because it is not believable, or sustainable. Again, it is apparent that too much praise at the cost of constructive criticism is unauthentic. That is where delivery of the message comes in.

## Feedback – It Is Not Always What You Say But How You Say It

Related to praise is the approach of how a message is delivered and this carries enormous weight. Messaging matters for every recipient and, especially our most highly sensitized individuals, those who experience anxiety and trauma. Messaging cannot be understated. How we deliver news matters and even more profoundly for our learners who struggle with distress.

Feedback, when it must be negative, can be conveyed in a more constructive and thoughtful manner, delivering it with calculated empathy. Create safety for children as recipients of criticism, even as you build your ratio of higher positive to negative feedback. Remember that one in five can and should still be criticisms, redirections, or negative reinforcement, where applicable.

Let us consider how much weight delivery and tone carry. Ahead in the Game (2012) anecdotally refers to evidence that examined two groups of participants. The first group was given positive performance feedback, by a superior who displayed negative non-verbal body language.

The second group were given negative performance feedback, but the supervisor was coached on messaging the news with a pleasant tone, more transparent body language and empathy. The results showed that the group receiving negative feedback, with a positive tone reported far more beneficial feelings about their meetings and wellbeing.

While this is an anecdotal reference, there is ample evidence available to support it. Adams (2017) provided more student specific reporting from the likes of trauma specialists, including Joyce Dorado, director of the Healthy Environments and Response to Trauma in Schools program at UC San Francisco.

She and other practitioners agree that teacher-student relationships involve a vital component – a teacher's voice and expression.

Koch (2017) found that the inflection elements of teachers' voices warrant consideration when preparing classroom instruction and for evaluating educational practice. This reinforces the anecdotal evidence that tone and delivery matter. Furthermore, as has been professed throughout, if it matters for a well-adjusted child, it matters even more for children impacted by trauma.

Furthermore, how you say it to students matters across the K-12 spectrum. In fact, in some ways, it may be even more profound for students in secondary school, because so much of the damage has already set in and students are more highly sensitized to their surroundings. Those surroundings include how and in what ways they are being communicated with, particularly with authority figures. Traumatized children often feel powerless over their surroundings.

Gooblar (2018) characterizes classroom instruction with older students, in much the same way. He emphasizes that tone is important when communicating with learners. The way we deliver our message to students is one of the most substantial ways we influence their learning environment; something that again greatly matters with children in distress.

*Teacher greeting at the door* . . . We have all stood in uncomfortable silence with other individuals in an elevator. The awkwardness of this moment is virtually universal and by no coincidence. Think about a moment when you walk into a store and the store clerk coldly peers over at you. The feeling that they detest you ushers in a sense of feeling unwelcome, with unwanted unease.

On the other hand, consider well-trained customer service staff who have learned the benefit of a friendly and pleasant greeting. They do not aim to swoop in and sell you something. Instead, a warm smile and pleasant body language tell you that you are welcome in this store, and their genuine nature can effectively and instantaneously put you at ease.

Back to our elevator. Many of us have experienced the humor of the moment when a cheerful individual contained within that small space for those brief moments makes a comment that we were all thinking, buckling the tension. A group chuckle follows, and an instant bond is forged among strangers, even for the briefest moment, until the door slides open and everyone ushers out into the frenzied space, possibly never to see each other again.

The realization that this interchange will play out may seem obvious. Yet understanding it and why interactions so often take this direction elicit in us our ability to use it in our efforts to connect with children. A teacher greeting at the door is something a principal had relentlessly promoted to his faculty, sometimes with exasperating frustration. Until he used science to show why it mattered.

After trying numerous ways to get teachers to greet students, from strong memos, to encouragement, pleading, to compliance, he turned to data. The administrator conducted a baseline, in which he measured time students vacated the hallways, and entered their teachers' classrooms. This resulted in some concerning, evidence that was obvious: the average hallway clearance time was 2.5 minutes *after* the bell to start class.

The principal shared this data with his teachers at the next faculty meeting and offered incentives for students and staff. He rallied a committee to promote the importance of being at classroom doors ready to learn on time, and the power of greeting kids at the door.

Through a professional development experience, the faculty were able to see that greeting the most disruptive and at-risk children at the door with a welcome message and encouragement to enter class substantially reduced their disruptive behaviors!

This school was able to excite an energy about getting students into classrooms and out of disruptive hallways, through a positive incentive-based program. It was a schoolwide effort, successfully orchestrated by one classroom teacher at a time. Following is how it worked.

## Pod Races

The school, like many middle schools is made up of teams, or groups, of content area teachers, called *houses*. Each house consists of the core subject areas: language arts, science, social studies, and math. Different levels of schools contain similar organizational structures. Elementary schools have grade level teams in different halls. High schools contain numerous departments in each wing. Therefore, everyone can enlist a similar schoolwide program, and team up areas of the school no matter the grade levels, or general school structure.

Pod races can be conducted during class changes throughout the day and times of each vary from one day to the next. This provides everyone the motivation and context to get to class, at different stages and transitions of the day. Hall areas and their associated classes that win are awarded *tickets* which go into a lottery for a drawing for each student and faculty earning the tickets.

## How It Changed Teacher–Student Relationships

Because students consistently arrive to class on time or within seconds of the bell, teachers get classes started sooner, avoid disruptions and have less disorderly conduct in the halls. Everyone has bought into this win-win situation. The principal posted the news that being on time to class meant saving 2.5 minutes per class, and the bigger payoff equaled a total of *eight school days saved* in a year. That is one simple way to maximize learning and improve school climate.

## The Payoff for All Students Including Those in Distress

You do not have to have a comprehensive positive behavior support system in place to employ this kind of positive reinforcement. The point is, make it about "winning together." Students and faculty are inspired by the competitive edge. They see it as a constructively positive contest.

Rewarding faculty alongside their students strengthens class-wide bonds between teachers and their students. It may not seem obvious, yet this is another role a teacher can play in gaining student trust, large scale, class wide. Wholescale trust opens the door for students impacted by the effects of trauma and anxiety. They become part of something larger (and safer) than themselves and their own lives. This is an example of promoting community, by working through something together. Teams that bond together learn how to work through problems together.

## Chapter Summary

Quick, effective interventions must be part of the teacher's practical toolkit, instruments that can be instituted seamlessly into daily classroom practice.

The two-minute intervention is a practical intervention when guided conferencing is integrated into the pre-existing environment. It is concise and focused.

The one-sentence intervention is even more concise, and most practical both for the teacher who cannot spend two minutes a day on designated children in distress, and in transferring the skill to children, as they develop their own narrative skills later.

The connection to one sentence ties into the one-sentence journal, which has been shown to literally help rewire the brain. That is power in efficient steady ways, and students can learn to use this as a tool in their recovery. If students are reluctant to write, or struggle with expressing themselves in writing, use online tools, like speech notes to help them transcribe.

Praise and getting the praise to criticism ratio right matters, and it means even more when helping children who are traumatized. As John Gottman demonstrates, a minimum of a 5:1 ratio of positives to negatives helps cultivate relationships. Teachers should be very aware of this ratio, and how often they issue praise, versus criticism as they develop the skills to issue praise in the right context and with authenticity.

While praise ratios are important, of equal value is how a message is delivered to students. Indeed, it has been evidenced that a message of constructive criticism can be delivered with fidelity more effectively than an inauthentic attempt or poorly delivered positive comment.

Teacher greeting at the door reduces conflict in schools, sets the tone for a positive welcome message by teachers to their students, and gets the most disruptive students to respond affirmatively to teacher efforts to get going at the important early moments of a class lesson.

# 6

# Formative Assessment – Establishing and Applying What Is Most Relevant

Summative and standardized assessments are often viewed as necessary evils in the context of measuring student progress. Data is necessary, in fact critical. Assessment is important to monitor a student's learning progress and ensure that instruction is being provided with fidelity. It enables educators to track student performance and challenge them. Summative assessment is an imperfect, if not critical and necessary diagnostic tool for evaluating student progress.

Yet exploration of techniques for more practical, highly authentic formative methods offer efficient, on the spot data collection. Shorter term formative practices allow the educator the opportunity to make more precise, localized, and targeted decisions, and to encourage children in a more incremental and time-responsive fashion. This has the effect of being more immediate, and relevant for learners in a world of short term, high speed information.

Guidelines proposed here exhibit the value of efficient and accurate real time assessment and the understanding that

DOI: 10.4324/9781003162971-6

summative assessments take too long to capture time sensitive support needs. Longer term assessments may also bear too negative a cost on learners already faced with the effects of trauma. Test anxiety impacts learners in ways that are exponentially more adverse for students impacted by distress.

An exploration of how and in which way shorter, more frequent assessments can be implemented, as a protocol, navigated by a menu of options is provided. Data applied to practices will be presented. These include an assembly of cost effective assessments that are already at the practitioner's disposal, and the coordination of incoming pieces of evidence.

## Pre-Existing Data Sets

Practitioners already have access to a tremendous amount of data from in-class student responses, within their everyday teaching practices. Teachers simply need to aggregate and organize pre-existing data into a cohesive fashion to tailor it for use in supporting their students. Real time data provide the teacher with trackable information that can and should be used more strategically, especially as children work toward post traumatic growth. Provided are examples of several methods that will be detailed for use of shorter-term data sets that are right under classroom teachers noses.

## Do Now Data Collection

A "Do Now" is an introductory activity, and teachers commonly use this prompt to warm up students as they settle into the class lesson. A Do Now is typically used to trigger students learning for the lesson, check in on a child's level of prior knowledge, and elicit recall of content understanding. This introductory exercise is effectively used when it sets the direction of the lesson for the teaching, drawing on student responses for context to teach from.

Science: Should We Bring Back Extinct Species?
Social Studies: What Does It Look Like To Stand Up For What's Right?
Health: Is It Healthier to Be a Vegetarian or an Omnivore?
Language Arts: How Can Schools Make Lunches More Appealing to Teens?

**FIGURE 6.1** Do Now Prompts

A Do Now is best integrated into classroom routine as it alerts students of the onset for student learning. Do Nows that are well developed and rehearsed are more efficient and increase student engagement. They are not expected to be lengthy introductions to the lesson. Opening activities are the initiation to the lesson and tend to set the stage for instruction.

A Do Now should take no more than eight to ten minutes for students to complete and for the teacher to assess student capacity for a targeted skill or lesson purpose. Figure 6.1 illustrates a few examples of Do Nows, which often serve like an essential question, priming student inquiry. Many more examples can also be found online.

## Exit Ticket (or Card) Activities

Teachers incorporate exit tickets to reveal what learners are thinking and what they have mastered during the class, at the closure of the lesson. Students must present an exit "ticket" to the teacher that they have completed with an answer to a question, a solution to a problem, or a response to what has been taught.

Exit Tickets help assess whether students can comprehend what has been taught. They allow the teacher to prepare for the next lesson based on what level of understanding students demonstrate. Exit activities help teachers make decisions for teaching and learning in the upcoming lesson. Figure 6.2 provides one example of exit tickets and more samples are easily available by searching online.

Exit cards and other lesson closures are good practice for gathering quick, authentic data on student progress. This is an excellent

---

**So What?** Have students answer this prompt: What takeaways from the lesson will be important to know three years from now? Why?

**Beat the Clock:** Ask a question. Give students 10 seconds to confer with peers before you call on a random student to answer. Repeat.

**Elevator Pitch:** Ask students to summarize the main idea in under 60 seconds to another student acting as a well-known personality who works in your discipline.

---

**FIGURE 6.2** Exit Ticket Prompts

opportunity to engage students in their raw self-reflection on learning and wellness. Notice that learning and wellness are (purposely) tagged together here. Often, we can elicit evidence of students' wellness, through their learning responses, and vice versa.

## Cataloging Do Nows and Exit Activity Data

Often, teachers use Do Now and exit activities to judge class wide comprehension in the moment. However, they do not necessarily employ this for either individualized practice, or to gather and track data over time. This is invaluable, purely raw, and formative information that adds a wealth of knowledge to the child's portrait of progress and challenge. Tracking these student responses and measuring them allows for both the recognition of student wellness and learning, and support for the next steps toward progress and small wins.

## Gamification Data Sets

Gamification is another popular tool teachers use to increase engagement, often to review for upcoming assessments. Yet the degree to which data is collected from these less formal, highly informative methods is lacking. Teachers often view gamification as a high interest tool to help students review for the assessment, and this is indeed one way to engage students in learning.

Yet gaming resources should also be used to collect information about student learning, and as a part of the progress monitoring methods for teachers to deploy. Gaming assessments like Kahoot, Nearpod, Plickers Pear Deck, and Flipgrid, along with online form collection resources are a few examples. Random name picker activities also serve to offer the teacher an equal and balanced way to select students. They are also a useful motivation for kids to "win" the chance to participate.

## Common Gaming Tools That Allow You to Aggregate Data

This is not an exhaustive list and is also tempered by the time in which this text was published. However, there are numerous gaming examples that allow you to access data locally from student responses that have stood the test of time. This section is presented to share these options and to remind the user of this guidebook that new and adapted models continue to evolve in the fast-changing world of the internet.

Other options exist, and the intent of this guide is not to provide an exhaustive list. Rather, these are offered as options to encourage the reader to adapt to or understand they can implement their own. Note that all options provided are free resources. It is important to mention that the reference to these resources is by no means an endorsement and the author is receiving no incentives for sharing them. They are simply common examples of many options for teachers to collect student data through gamification and form aggregation, useful in building a repository of student information to support their post traumatic development.

Kahoot is one of the most recognized gaming tools teachers engage in with their classes, especially for review. They are simple to set up, easy to share and engaging for learners. Teachers can expand their use of this as a review or pre-assessment tool to gather information on student performance. A quick navigation over to Kahoot's support center helps you find instructions on how to get reports with results of your challenges (Kahoot, 2021).

Nearpod (n.d.) is another commonly used gaming tool that can serve as a collection mechanism. It can be interactive, collaborative, and offer gaming type quizzes. Nearpod formative assessments allow the teacher real time tracking of student responses, including polling, open ended questions and more.

Nearpod (2020) allows the teacher to upload previously organized power points, slides, and videos, which a teacher can input questions directly into for each. Pre-made lessons are also available for use, or the teacher may adapt their own. The teacher has the choice to execute a Nearpod activity in real time, or assign it for independent work, and to control the pace.

To download data collected in Nearpod:

1. In the My Library section, select the Reports tab.
2. Reports of student responses are populated, select the one you wish to access.
3. The opening reports screen displays a summary of your students' participation – these list student names, their overall and individual responses to each question.
4. Within the desired screen report, select Download in the upper toolbar, as a CSV (a basic excel spreadsheet), or pdf format. You can collect all responses, or on "student view," just one student's responses.
5. Responses will be revealed for the teacher offline in reader only view and online for use, tracking and manipulation of student performance.

Plickers is a useful tool for the teacher on the run. For instance, teachers who cannot wait for, or do not have access to student devices, such as in a physical education class, or on a field trip, or in another field-based experience can gather data using Plickers. It is cost effective because of the easy access teachers can pull, right from their cell phone. They simply download the app, print out student response cards on plain printer paper (you can laminate these to resist weathering), and scan student responses as they are held up.

Plickers enables the teacher to download a spreadsheet of student responses, identified by name. It has limitations, such as only allowing for multiple choice responses. Yet this is a useful way to gather quick data, and check for student understanding, as well as state of mind, when teachers see the need for a check in with their learners. Responses are collected individually, and as a group, allowing for class wide inspection, or individual students. Search Plickers on YouTube for how to set it up.

Pear Deck has similar features to Nearpod in that it allows the teacher to present material, engage learners to interact and provide responses to and track these for student progress monitoring purposes. Once signed up for an account, go through the process of allowing Pear Deck to connect to your Google drive.

To get the data:

1. From the home screen, click on Review Sessions.
2. End Session (3 dots) – you can always reopen this.
3. Another option is to click Export to Spreadsheet and your Google drive will house student responses, automatically saved in your Google Drive in the *Pear Deck > Exports* folder. All spreadsheet exports are saved there. Objective answers are viewable here (multiple choice, true/false, scalable responses, etc.).

Flipgrid is a video recording and archiving lesson response system. This is useful for documenting student oral responses from a discussion, critical viewpoints, debate position, presentation practice, or to express feelings. These can be easily downloaded, and stored, to online drives like Google and OneDrive that are housed by the school. These are useful as video portfolios and popular among language teachers, engaging students in presentation and oral language skills. Here are some basic instructions for using Flipgrid:

1. Sign up for an account and share with students.
2. Students record video as prompted.
3. Students are prompted to submit their response and offered the option to download. This video is also sent to the teacher.
4. The download feature allows direct download on the computer, or in a linked Google Drive account, for student portfolio storage.
5. The student can share the video with a teacher with editing access or make the teacher the video owner.

Be sure to rename files downloaded for appropriate cataloguing and more efficient retrieval (student name, date, class, etc.).

Online form collections are free and easy to use in both Google and Microsoft. For the scope of this text, Google forms will be discussed yet Microsoft forms offer the same practical value. Use what works for you. Setting up a Google form is easy to follow, by browsing any recent (within the past year) YouTube video explanation or by accessing the Google support site. Once student responses are collected, it is recommended the teacher use Google's built in interface to create a Google spreadsheet.

To view responses to your Form, first,

1. Open your Drive and locate the Google Form.
2. From there, you can view student responses as a summary or individually.
3. Open it. Navigate to the Responses tab. You will see a small green spreadsheet icon next to responses. Click on this and it prompts you to create a new spreadsheet, which automatically populates your responses.

The critical component in all pre-existing data sources is to collect and measure student progress by using this data and making decisions based on it. Collections of data sets help guide decision making in supporting students. If students are showing progress, we are prepared to celebrate and encourage their direction forward. This is the premise of small wins psychology. Students experience an overall upward trajectory. Even as normal setbacks occur and appear on a graph, the prevalence of direction is forward, like a trending stock market chart.

## How to Gather Data During Real Time Instruction

Several strategies are offered for data collection in real time. Do not consider this a limited or fixed set. Other ideas may emerge and can often be driven by community context. These are universal measures that work toward the concept of stacking methods together. That is, the more you combine, the greater the compound effect that results from integrating multiple methods. Standalone ideas are certainly effective, but more limited in scope.

Consider the risk of "putting all your eggs in one basket." Alternatively, adopt a series of workable solutions, adding to the advantage that results when one idea does not work, more ideas will likely work together due to their overall effect. Following are a series of recommended methods, common in schools, and easily replicable. Again, this list is not exhaustive, rather it is instructive and encourages consideration for adding to your own best practices.

### Conferencing

Conferencing is a skill employed commonly by teachers, in the many numerous informal and ongoing interactions they engage in, all day. Often when conferences occur, a wealth of information is accessible, if practitioners are looking in the right direction. Without a plan for attention to the details that emerge during

mini conferences, a tremendous amount of formative information regarding student profiles is lost.

Conferencing is typically situated in the pretext of teacher
check ins and clarification of content presented. Developing
skills to fine tune collection of student responses is a worthy
undertaking. Teacher-student interactions should not be unend-
ing. Often, students will reveal what is on their minds without
a teacher struggling to obtain the information, through natural
discourse.

Aside from the curricular benefits, and with an attention
toward aiding students when they are distressed, conferencing
offers numerous advantages. First, this practice can guide students in their self-reflection; a critical learning proficiency that
aims to challenge students higher level processing and reflection. Additionally, the teacher can offer help and provide needed
advice, something that is naturally integrated into conferencing
interactions.

Students disclose both discreetly and overtly, often in their
writing. Teachers can use student passages as their baseline
for the conference. Specifically, geared questions can be used
as probes to check for progress. Systematic collection of data
points from these conferences and analysis can and should be
adapted as more coordinated ways to employ progress monitoring techniques.

## Approach to Conferences

Find the most opportune moments when kids are working independently. This allows for the class to work at a productive noise
level while the teacher naturally engages students individually.
Do Now and project-based work times serve this function. Consider room location – a spot in the room that is private enough,
yet still allows the teacher to see her other students. The teacher
can check on the class and simultaneously be eye level with the
student in the conference.

Structure these times. Having three to five-minute conferences with every child allows you to rotate through students at a rate of approximately a week and a half, each. Assign students specific days when they will have their personalized conference. This allows learners to feel prepared, valued, informed, and attended to.

Conferences can be arranged for a variety of reasons and students are typically familiar with the practice, so it should not come across as fabricated. They can be constructed to guide students to learn specific skills, especially as a strategy to work on gap skills; such as areas students need extra attention in.

During the conference, guided reflection questions can help students think in terms of their own progress. These are authentic opportunities to engage students both in curricular skill areas, and their overall well-being. Additionally, an "evaluation" conference can be used for students to measure their own mastery. This is an opportunity to chart and track progress. In this context, students get to develop the skill of making their own judgments. Finally, two-minute interventions were discussed earlier in this text. Conferences provide the ideal scenario for this quick intervention.

## Pre- and Post-Unit Reflection Surveys

Survey is a helpful method for allowing students to respond electronically and can measure in shorter time bursts what they know before content is presented, to compare with knowledge gained after instruction. This is one of the best ways to show progress and encourage students to see their upward trajectory. Pre-assessments typically expose gaps, which are well covered after presentation of materials and this noticeable difference has a positive spin for the student seeing their progress in the mastery of their own knowledge.

Adjustments can be made based on the depth and speed of knowledge acquisition. This can even be incorporated into the student's Individualized Learning Plan (ILPs), a plan that measures their individual progress. ILPS will be discussed in greater depth in Chapter 8. Reflection surveys are also detailed in Chapters 7 and 8, where goal setting is necessary to set the path forward for a child's individual progress.

## Data Collection

Shorter, more frequent quizzes promise better acquisition by learners than their summative counterparts (Paul & Paul, 2015). Breaking up learning and measurement of progress, like all goal setting establishes more manageable, achievable outcomes by learners. There are many opportunities for this to take place. These are already occurring, such as in the use of gamification discussed earlier and like the conferencing point, much of this data is lost, because it is being looked at too narrowly.

Practitioners can use resources already in place to examine and use data to inform their understanding of student progress, and wellness. They can leverage these for the benefit of the learner. This includes charting, demonstrating student progress and reinforcing their development, as well as identifying areas of need and tailoring support to individual learners.

## Instituting the Assessments – Type, Duration, Challenge Level, Frequency, Where and When

This chapter offers practical approaches to institute short assessments. These include an understanding of the type, duration, challenge level, and frequency of the data gathered. Further exploration includes the hands-on, tactical value of technology to collect and organize data intended to help learners grow and develop quickly and efficiently.

A general rationale for why formative assessments are ideal to use is that they make quick, targeted and meaningful assessment available, collected and tracked over time. Next, this guidebook offers specific types and examples of each, in ways that can apply to subject areas, or for general implementation and use.

## Do Now and Exit Activities

Do Nows and exit activities were presented earlier as the basis for an introductory and exit activity to the lesson. Quick and useful example types include *Essential Questions (ES),* a primer tool for immediately gauging a student's response and understanding, that provides a purpose within the ES. The ES prompt or closure can be performed by students individually, or in partnered work.

Essential questions are developed for the purpose of encouraging deeper thought and discussion about a relevant topic. They are framed to provoke robust and abstract dialogue about the content rather than much more concrete, closed-ended responses. Consider that an essential question presents a *good* versus a *Google* question. It is subjective and open ended, rather than a short and closed response to the inquiry.

In other words, you cannot just "Google the answer," that demands in depth perspective and thought, even as an isolated inquiry for students to respond to. An example of an ES versus a Google question might be: "Why is the topic of the electoral college such a controversial one," versus "how many electoral college votes are required for a president to be elected?"

While the essential question can be issued to students as a check of prior understanding, it can also be implemented for the purpose of checking prior knowledge before instruction begins. Therefore, Do Nows can serve to quickly assess comprehension of previously introduced material or be presented as a gauge to assess prior knowledge of newly presented material. Likewise, exit cards offer a check of mastery following instruction, informing teachers of student readiness on content that is presented.

Therefore, Do Now and exit activities serve to provide preparation for discussion in the pending lesson and build a background of foundation and insight to check back with a closure prompt. A text passage is provided for students to read, followed by multiple choice and/or open-ended questions. Student answers on these checks are a way to signal the direction of and what about the upcoming assignment it will be.

Another example of Do Now and exit activities is to serve as a reading check to determine whether students understand the material and possibly as an audit to see if they have done the reading in preparation for class. If arranged the right way, this may help to incentivize learners to perform the assignment. A quick-check method allows the teacher to examine student responses to both objective (example, multiple choice) and subjective (example open ended) response types.

## Track Learning Over Time

Having students respond to a prompt at the beginning of the lesson or unit on a Post-It Note, a teacher may be inclined to illicit the same response entered in a shared document online. Storage of these responses from students, especially monitored over time offers sustainable value. Students can post responses, either on an actual anchor chart, or a virtual message or cork board. It would be advisable to digitize this experience to track responses over time.

At the close of the lesson, or unit, students can respond to the same ES prompt on a different colored Post-It, or on a post forum via a shared form. Collecting responses to a form allows the practitioner to chart the responses, and to manipulate the data from a spreadsheet, where responses are distributed to. For visual monitoring, have students place their end of lesson entry right next to their first entry so that they can compare how their thinking has evolved.

If the teacher is employing digital sources, the acquisition of pre- and post-responses from a Google or Microsoft form can serve as a visual representation like Post Its on an anchor chart, and they are saved digitally for later access for analysis. The responses are transmitted from form to spreadsheet. Programs can aggregate this information for the teacher and chart progress for student and teacher reference. A couple of quick examples to illustrate the ease of this charting and tracking follow.

## Charting a Course to Tracking Student Pre- and Post-Response Data

Form collection that is distributed to a spreadsheet allows the teacher several ways to store and track the data. Charting the responses for transparent disclosure to the student is almost always a sensible way to inform students about their performance. One way to do this is from a Google spreadsheet disseminated to documents via tools that take a few quick steps to generate into an individualized format.

Personalizing the document for each child supports the model espoused in this text that there is no prescription that works best for all. Collection of student-specific data enables the teacher to differentiate by tracking learners pre- and post-performance on a trajectory. One example of a quick resource to do this with is a spreadsheet extension contained within Google, called "Save as Doc." Appendix E provides instructions for how to execute the simple steps for use with this tool.

For a basic understanding, the educator employing this technique should know that any pre-and post-form prompts are fed into a Google spreadsheet. The spreadsheet is connected to an extension referred to as Save as Doc. This extension allows the user to include headings.

The student data is fed into the document, offering a personalized approach and experience for the viewer tracking and charting their progress. An instructional for how to use this resource can be found online ("'Save as Doc' Google Sheets Add on, How to use," 2020, 03:15–05:21).

Bear in mind that tools like Save as Doc are dynamically changing, so the process or access to it could change its availability at any time. The point is, these kinds of resources are everywhere, yet ever changing and knowing this means practitioners should be prepared to adjust to these changes, to adapt to new models, or choose to employ data collection methods that are more enduring. One of these is a time-tested method called mail merge.

## Mail Merge Programs

Mail merge has been around as long as Windows-based software has and, a quarter century later, it remains an effective distribution tool. This is especially beneficial when tracking and charting a student's individual progress. Illustrating this in a personalized format from mail merge makes the information authentic and tangible for learners and their teachers.

There are many mail merge programs, with origins in Microsoft extending to Google and other online sources. For purposes of commonality and accessibility, the Windows-based program that connects a spreadsheet to a word document, tailored to the individual student is the recommended (though not limited to being the only) source.

Mail merge programs are reliable, sustaining ways to collect and report student responses. Yet they take time to arrange. Is the time worth it? To put this important question into context, picture a restaurant buffet. To the customer, a buffet appears to make the job of the waitress look simple, easy. Yet, like an ant colony busy working underground, the work behind the scenes, the processes to set up the foundation for successful execution is often hidden beneath the surface.

However, the payoff is well worth it. This is reliant on the preferences of the reader to choose. A beautifully laid out display of food, accentuated by smart placement and garnishes make the hard work behind the scenes well worth it.

Likewise, setting up a mail merge is a valued resource to arrange communication of tracking and data monitoring. Instruction for how to set up a mail merge to monitor student data sets and information are available on YouTube, at Microsoft and third-party sites. One reliable option is *Mail Merge from Excel to Microsoft Word* (2020, 03:15–05:21).

Remember that one method is not an end all. Consider your options. Numerous choices, previously mentioned, and those that follow are viable alternatives. Just know the value mail merge has to offer, like a rich buffet spread, that can set the stage for a well-executed data tracking resource.

## Online Programs

Programs which are accessible in a cloud-based or online format are viable in contemporary storage and for access of student database collections. Most school communities invest in student management systems, which allow for access to data, but these are universal grading systems. Many do not contain the authentic and readily available anecdotal data sources that can be informative in our work toward identifying more targeted student performance and needs, both academically and social-emotionally.

Student management systems primarily offer the ability to access performance-based assessment, graded assignments, with limited qualifying information about these assessments. Therefore, it is sensible to pull this data to track global performance over time. Yet the true telling is in the day to day, formative, short-term authentic student responses.

Most online systems present concerns about sustainability, and the practitioner is better off using known and longstanding, as well as online programs which offer offline access of information. One online alternative which is available, yet not typically used in a true data collection approach, is student interactive responses boards.

## Downloadable Messages From Interactive Boards, Padlet

Interactive boards are everywhere online, and the variety can be overwhelming, as well as wide ranging in quality. Many are freemium models, which operate on the premise of carrot and stick: we will give you the basics and dangle other premium features, but you must pay for the extras. This guidebook maintains that there are plentiful free or low-cost resources that are reliable and sustainable, for teacher and student access over time.

Due to this plethora of options, the decision to refer to resources remains exclusively based on how children can have the impacts of their trauma remedied. Examples serve to illustrate one of a variety of available sources, especially with free and low cost online services. These are dynamic, subject to change; availability can also change, and others can quickly pop up anew. Teachers should frame their approach with this understanding, so they can be prepared to adapt.

Having established the principle that products characterized in this text may serve as a model for many options, one popular product that functions as a useful online board is Padlet. This resource allows the teacher to facilitate interactive experiences that go beyond the traditional post-it on the easel approach. These are lively, interactive learning activity boards, yet often teachers end their use there. That is a disservice to the data sources made available on students from inputs, and the ability for teachers to collect functional follow up for use of this data that Padlet-like online tools can account for.

While tools like Padlet (2021) serve numerous functions, its most known and useful purposes are the creation of an online post board that can be shared between teacher and student, student to student, group, and class wide. A unique Padlet link for the "wall" is generated that remains accessible if the teacher keeps access open. Access can be public, by invitation to students only, or private and the board site allows collaborators to insert ideas, images, video, sounds, and more.

Collecting this information via virtual posts or boards, allows the teacher to download responses in multiple formats: via spreadsheet, pdf, or as an image. The ability to edit makes spreadsheet conversion ideal. Remember mail merge too, when considering this option. Again, this is choice driven, based on teacher and school preference. Presented here are guided suggestions to consider.

Some may prefer the pdf format that allows for teacher warehousing of student artifacts, such as in a child's digital portfolio. However, for purposes regarding the scope of this text, the ability to transform spreadsheet responses into accessible and manipulable analysis tools is recommended. This format allows for current, and future reference. It fosters the ability to track responses over time and easily manipulate and update data for reference and analysis.

### Assessment

As students complete Do Nows, exit and other formative activities, teachers can collect informal, anecdotal data on performance to modify the upcoming instruction. Alternatively, teachers can use the completed formative data to construct leveled flexible groups. Arranging students into groups allows the teacher to zone in on identifiable skill groups.

The advantage of mapping subgroups is that homing in on their learning and wellness needs increases efficiency of focus in working with students. Likewise, time is managed more systematically. Assessment then should continue to be an important instrument for data tracking and monitoring of student progress in the three-step process.

## Chapter Summary

Use of formative assessment is called for throughout this text. It has been established that this is a more informal, feasible real time method for gaining important information about student development.

Pre-existing data sets are already available to teachers. What they need to do differently to effectively use them for the three-step method is how they organize and access this data.

Do Nows and exit activities offer introductory and closure tasks that provide a tremendous amount of data in snippets that teachers can access to consider student responses and use for tracking their progress.

Gamification is something frequently used by teachers, especially when they are reviewing for an assessment, or to increase engagement of their learners during instruction. Gamification offers valuable data that can be accessed, downloaded, stored, and referenced for decision making. Various tools are included in gaming collection, but the teacher should not consider these as delimiters. Rather, they are exemplars that can be used, or variations of sources to be tapped.

Kahoot is among the most popular games and has a vehicle to collect data from performance response.

Nearpod offers a presentation style method for engaging students in interactive activities, which prompt them for responses, to be collected.

Plickers is a one device tool ideal for collecting digital data when multiple devices are not available, or you are out in the field with learners, collecting their responses.

Peardeck (n.d.) operates like Nearpod, in teacher presentation and prompt for student responses that can be collected.

Flipgrid offers an intuitive audiovisual collection device that works well for archiving student video responses in a digital portfolio format to track their performance over time.

Form collection allows for collecting student responses in a common, free and easy way to distribute this data to spreadsheets that allow for teachers to take that data and sort and analyze it.

Conferencing offers teachers a practical and more personalized method for collecting student responses and using the conference to engage learners in our support of them.

Using sorting tools like Save as Doc, mail merge and post it collection allows for teachers to construct a catalog of student response in a clean and accessible manner. This includes online post instruments, like Padlet, which are also downloadable.

Assessment offers formative data that we can use to monitor and inform about student progress in the three-step process.

# 7

# Goal Setting – Small Wins Psychology and Why It Matters

The practitioner is now equipped with the tools for tackling trauma and amassing a collection of data about their students. Recall that this is done through an unobtrusive collection of information. The next important phase is to aid the child in their goal setting process. The critical recognition of small wins built over time can now be initiated.

The rationale that "small wins" psychology can propel individuals to true success is well documented. As opposed to large grandstanding plans focused on landmark achievements, the learner is celebrated strategically, authentically, and incrementally. The true degree to which recognition of the small win is delivered connects the relevance of celebration of worthiness to the small achievement, or win.

While the literature clearly demonstrates the psychological power and benefit of small wins, there is a surprisingly limited set of research specific to students. Most of the available evidence is based on business models and linked to adult milestones, not students. For instance, The Progress Principle

DOI: 10.4324/9781003162971-7

(2011) was based on research among organizational managers. Amabile and Kramer (2011) similarly addressed "The Power of Small Wins," in relation to the structures of the corporate world.

Corporate entities were focused on how companies generate successes built on prior accomplishments. While the psychological power of association and confidence building most certainly provide sound rationale, publishers concentrated on broader contexts for corporations. Absent from the literature were connections to the advantages schools and children could benefit from this as an operating principle.

More recently at TEDx Chilliwack (2018) the topic of small wins was presented. Additionally, a blog by Rob Smith, "How to make your small wins work for you" (2019), reinforces small wins psychology. Provided were practical processes for why and how small wins work and can be so beneficial to the individual psyche when working toward a goal or overcoming personal challenges. Still, none of these referred to developmental work with children, nor with learners trying to rebuild from their traumatic experiences.

This seems surprising. How could effective psychology on human achievement appear so lacking for those who could benefit from it the most? Our most fragile, at risk children face daunting struggles with their undeveloped minds and trauma, warranting a connection to small wins psychology. Granted, parallel concepts of goal setting are commonly practiced in education, and with young learners. Even 12-step programs for addicts present a similar logic, but this is not focused on children.

Yet the simplicity and quick effectiveness of small wins psychology is clearly an area that must be given greater attention, and we begin with this field guide. This supportive model for children will be developed as this text seizes on that gap. It offers to present the unique interaction for traumatized learners between relationship building, tracking of progress, and celebrating small wins.

The rationale considers application of small wins at least as important to aid students recovery efforts, and even more so with children who are working against the effects of trauma. By nature of the way positive behavior programs and interventions are instituted and with an alluring degree of success, these programs exercise reinforcing tactics. Yet the use of small wins will be outlined in much greater detail and demonstrate how practicing this as a strategy works.

Small wins matter remarkably to traumatized individuals because the long-term success, a focus on large-scale achievement is so daunting, feels so unattainable, distant, and unreachable. Yet McMinn (2017) presents small wins in the context of shifting in the right direction by effecting change with simple and concrete steps, as straightforward as making your own bed. Consider the psychological edge of these subtle, tiny milestones. The progress principle (Amabile & Kramer, 2011) illustrates this, with the ripple effect caused by starting small, and expanding with steady, seemingly unremarkable yet deliberately progressive steps toward breakthroughs.

In the school context, a guided facilitator or teacher enables the child to develop goals along a continuum that sets the stage for manageable, successive, linear progressions. Along the way, the teacher fosters a method for re-evaluating these steps. This is particularly important when following short, frequent intermittent mini assessments while monitoring student progress.

Additionally, this allows for the development of the small wins that students can visualize in a very concrete sense. Remember that small wins are progressive, acting in the form of an ever-expanding wave. If one starts, often, a second and additional waves or "wins" cascade toward the progress we aim to see in students.

Since many children benefit from visual cues, one method for demonstrating their progress in a tangible and recognizable way is by providing a chart for tracking to show the path they travelled, and where they continue to move forward to. Additionally, like checking off a list, this has the effect of allowing the child to experience firsthand what they have accomplished regarding the task. This yields an order that shows students how they are moving along a continuum. As you can imagine, this is a visually encouraging albeit simplistic perspective.

One of the factors that distinguishes successful individuals from unsuccessful ones is the way in which they respond to the perceived gap between setbacks and where they are situated with their overall progress. Those who see regressions as a part of progress have come to understand that no path to success is met with perfection as in a straight line upward. In fact, individuals who respond well to any regression understand that it is impossible to have a setback without having already demonstrated some success, and vice versa.

This is a profound realization in helping a traumatized individual tip the scale toward a cycle that forges a developmental path. Getting them there takes patience and encouragement. It is an intricate balance and small wins simply must outnumber setbacks, a viable goal for students to see that they are not stuck. Rather, they are visibly forging ahead with the power to understand that they can influence their own result far more than they may grasp.

Traumatized individuals who suffer from the impact of their distress can persevere beyond their fate, if they develop an understanding that is nurtured by the educators and adults around them. Historically, this has been referred to as a person's internal locus of control (Rotter, 1954). That is, learners who view their success or failure as a result of the effort and hard work they put forth impact their outcome from within, not being dictated to by extenuating circumstances that surround them.

## Growth Versus Fixed Mindset

Educational researchers popularized the concept of growth mindset in the early part of this millennia (Dweck, 2006). As opposed to a fixed mindset, a growth mindset is an outlook in which the most fundamental skills can be developed through effort rather than a presupposed talent. This creates a strong desire for learning and a resilience that is a prerequisite for success. Examples of fixed mindset versus growth mindset include assuming you are *no good at math* (fixed), versus *I didn't do well on that math test, but if I keep practicing, I will get better* (growth).

No one can sustain staying in a growth mindset, all the time. This is on par with no one having the capacity to constantly move forward, without expecting some setbacks along the way. Part of the challenge is how our primal brain thought processes interfere, engineered to place doubt in our minds as protective instincts from our ancient cognitive defense mechanisms. Learning how to reverse-engineer this with signposts, like small wins and mindfulness are some of the key tools to master the right outlook and forge ahead.

The importance of disrupting the sense of defeat quickly, by having visible signs of advances and seeing what works by being readily accessible cannot be understated. Positive Behavior Support in Schools (PBSIS) techniques like the program sponsored by Rutgers University, which offers simple, yet thoughtful techniques implement such strategies. One example among PBSIS techniques is the ratio of praise to criticism, previously discussed. This can help teachers tip the realization of their learners toward positive, growth mindset thinking, rather than negative self-talk that festers in the fixed, primal state.

## Charting Small Wins

To make progress visible to students, small wins should be tracked at data points, so that those incremental progressions are documented, and available for later reference. Making this illustrated, perhaps even color coordinated in a simplistic, easy to read view is beneficial to the child. You may wonder, but what if the child does not progress and they see greater negatives on the chart? Wouldn't that create a reverse effect, further damaging a child's already fragile mindset and impair their ability to persevere?

This is where the skill and psychological understanding of a teacher comes into play. Every great teacher knows that perception is more powerful than fact. In delivering the news, be thoughtful that you can find success in any small measure, and document this on the child's chart. This is not to suggest watering down the achievement, rather it is to get the child through those tough spots and see overall progress, the big picture. Everyone at some point has better days, and eventually a series of those will come along. For those slower, and more difficult earlier moments, be creative!

Examples of getting through the tough spots include global goalpost reviews ("see where you were versus how far you have come?") and micro milestone achievements. For instance, if a child correctly answers a teacher orchestrated prompt (you know they will get the answer right, or you have prepared them), celebrate with encouragement and praise, just always remain authentic.

Simple Excel and Google sheets allow for the creation of a win-loss chart. Use these and monitor them regularly, with set points and allowances provided for celebration and reward. Begin in smaller shorter bursts, and eventually space these out as the child begins to demonstrate more sustained and broader progress. These moments for reward and praise can be integrated into conferences, as discussed previously.

Shakespeare suggested that *nothing is ever good or bad but thinking it makes it so*. Understanding the power of how we speak to ourselves and why this influences our success or failure in moving through challenges makes a difference. Self-talk and how this can profoundly impact a child who is dealing with trauma weighs significantly on our capacity to provide a support network for them.

Facilitation of goal setting and small wins helps the child to recognize that they have an avenue toward success, and that this path should be followed both despite and possibly because of their trauma. This is where post traumatic growth aims to aid in our traumatized youth's progress. Self-talk plays a significant role in this approach. Negative self-talk is instinctive, positive self-talk is practiced. Understanding this helps shape awareness and conscious practice.

Distanced self-talk (Shpancer, 2020) is a concept that functions to remove the person and his emotions from the problem. This method engages the learner in reflecting on their distress from an outside perspective. Incorporating distanced self-talk is accomplished by a change of pronouns. Essentially, the individual achieves this separation by incorporating talk that is executed in the third person. Do this by having them replace their name, using pronouns "he, she, they," or by observing the concern, with a fly on the wall perspective.

For example, when you examine a personal challenge, consider phrasing it as, How is Mike feeling about this problem? or *How will "he" resolve this issue?* or, *What's the 'fly on the wall' outlook on what transpired?* Separating self is the key element in this conscious language of distanced self-talk. It effectively dissociates the person long enough, as if to see from the outside looking in, in a way that liberated the person to objectively measure with greater logic.

Consider a personalized statement like *Oh, my god, how am I going to do this? I can't get this paper done in one night without help. It takes days for me to put something like this together!* When statements are depersonalized, we replace "I" and "me" with "you" or their own names and say things like, *Seth, you can do this. You've prepared for assignments like this before and you know where to find the information.*

The reason this works is because we typically use third person language to refer to other people. This depersonalizes the reference to oneself, and reinforces a less intimate, more objective (and fair) viewpoint. Consider the contrasting statements by Seth. The first is what a child might normally say to himself, followed by the switch to distanced self-talk. The brain processes distanced self-talk in a way that helps the person step outside himself, at least long enough to use the reasoning that allows for higher level cognitive rationale.

## Post-Traumatic Growth: Strategy and Direction

### The Wound Is the Place Where the Light Enters You. – Rumi

It might seem contrary to logic to assume that pain and suffering could lead to growth and success. Yet following are two historic examples that have reinforced the rationale that scientists and psychologists demonstrate why post-traumatic growth can and does work. Rumi, an ancient Persian poet, pointed this out when he wrote about injury, deciding to use this to one's advantage.

Rumi understood, a millennia ago, that when life is always positive, it is easy to lose sight of spirituality, yet when pain occurs, we often reach into our spiritual bag, searching for a deeper sense of self. When reflection and looking inward is stimulated, we search for a sense of what is happening, and discover ways to manage the pain. Rumi's "wound" is a representation of hardship individuals encounter, that facilitates deep reflection.

Pain can be the source of insight about a person's challenges. It is in times of suffrage, that we have the opportunity to draw on our reserve of strength and figure out ways to deal with pain. This is the catalyst for growing stronger. A person's true potential is measured by reaching deeper to push through and to go further, beyond their limits until they reach an upper limit. This limit is not normally tested in times of comfort. Consider this as you read the two intriguing scenarios about those who persevered remarkably beyond suffrage and demonstrated post-traumatic growth.

Google found that their most effective workers were not graduates of upper echelon universities. Instead, the most successful were those who had overcome a tragic loss in their lives and had been able to translate that distress into growth

(Ismail, Malone, Geest, & Diamandis, 2014). Profound personal loss culminated in people who were humbler and more open to learning, producing more effective employees. These attributes can be the space needed to forge willingness, creativity, and persistence.

A historical and longitudinally proven case study shows similar results, dating to the early 1940s. World War II was well underway, and millions were suffering from the brutal terror of the Nazi regime. Many had their lives ended senselessly. Others were treated insufferably. The fact that many survived, often through shocking and courageous stories of heroism was a miracle. The outlook was dim. Yet Holocaust survivors generally far exceeded expectations, more often leading to remarkable, and dignified lives.

They became extraordinary success stories. The predictions were often dim. How could anyone recover from the kind of terror inflicted as had been on these victims? Yet, they did; having families, successful careers, and many migrated to liberty in places like America. They became significant and contributing members of society, despite all the tragedy and terror they faced.

How was this all possible? How could those who were exposed to years of horror and inhumane treatment not only survive, but thrive? Holocaust survivors thrived not despite but often because of their distress. They worked through, maneuvering into amazing post-traumatic lives; successes that outshined many medical professionals' prediction of what was to become of them.

Consider that some concluded many from the Holocaust era would be better off sheltered, even institutionalized. That did not happen. Instead, they lived their lives, and experienced post traumatic growth. This may have seemed impossible. But think about those heroic survivors.

Certainly, their stories could have, maybe should have ended in tragedy, sadly predicted by many "experts" to end in misery. At the finish line of World War II, Winston Churchill famously said, "Never waste a good crisis." In the maddening destruction of a devastating world war, he had the audacity to draw this conclusion. Little did those living through that dark time know today just how intuitive his infamous quote and the meaning behind it was. Indeed, this was a bold statement that remains timeless and proven, now by facts from traumatized Google employees and Holocaust survivors alike.

Psychological research has shown with proof that Churchill's intuition was spot on. The suffering caused by traumatic events can be repurposed as a strength, one that perpetuates opportunities for self-improvement and success, rather than destruction and defeat. This is not fiction. There is science that history has demonstrated evidence of this fact.

For those warning that children living through learning in the Covid-19 era would damage them forever, point to the amazing lives Holocaust survivors led. The author was blessed to meet one such survivor in 2010. This survivor was in his 80s and had the most incredible gratitude he had ever witnessed. While the survivor shared tales of horror and survival, he focused far more on themes of gratitude, and opportunity. He got to live, to grow, to become something larger than his trauma. He, like so many among him was an inspiration.

Like the holocaust survivor and the many more whose stories are passed down from generation to generation, we know that students endured difficult circumstances during Covid-19. We respect that this felt unfair to them. It is unfair. They should have enjoyed this part of their childhood, experiencing the innocence that is supposed to go along with it. With post-traumatic growth, children can learn that they have a choice: to wallow in their sorrow about their circumstance or decide that they should never waste a good crisis.

This perspective is not presented to minimize the tragedy and challenge children face. Rather it is a gentle push to remind them to use it as a learning experience like no other. It is a way to appreciate what one has, what all of us can return to, and how they have and will persist, beyond and because of the challenges that they endured during difficult times.

If there is any doubt, remember to look at the science that individuals like Churchill had, the foresight to accurately portray beyond the devastation of trauma. He may have had the extraordinary perspective to recognize what lies beyond terror. Yet the real inspirations are the millions of Holocaust survivors who went on with their lives, after the fire dimmed, and the light from a new beginning arose. Likewise, research from Google employees who experienced trauma and became among the best workers proved the same.

Like the gap that exists regarding small wins and strategy to support children, post-traumatic growth techniques are nearly absent from the literature. One small blog posted by Miller (2018) proposes ideas for guiding youth through post-traumatic growth. There may be broader research that offers effects of post-traumatic growth, yet strategy implementation is virtually absent. That will be considered here, with research showing what has been tested in the field and anecdotal experiences showing time-tested practices.

Post-traumatic growth techniques should not be viewed as methods for operating in isolation from other factors presented in this text, such as small wins psychology. Recall the synergy characterized in the three-step process represented within the framework that guides this resource. Every approach should work in integrated ways, to compound the effects, with more strength. Certainly, doing so tactically points the child in a meaningful direction, one that fosters opportunity through mechanisms like positive self-talk, and the brain's ability to process stories.

## Story Therapy

Stories serve as a powerful therapeutic variant because they offer an escape into the mind. The feeling that you are living through the experience when engrossed in a story is the reason we are so captivated by a good story. A story conveyed successfully is so profound that speakers' and listeners' brains demonstrate cognitive connectedness.

This may sound like science fiction, like a Star Trek mind meld, but let us understand how this connectedness works. When experiencing a well-composed story, the exact same areas of the brain light up on an MRI in both the storyteller and her listener, simultaneously. When you listen to a great story, your brain literally mirrors the brain of the storyteller. Consider it this way: when you hear a story you are deeply engaged in, your brain responds as if it is truly experiencing the event itself. That is why story therapy can be so helpful to learners impacted by trauma, as they experience stories of hope, inspiration, and resilience.

Story therapy is a psychotherapeutic method that by nature of its qualification, may make some considering the technique in day-to-day operations seem impractical. Teachers are not trained psychologists, as readily acknowledged throughout this field guide. Yet one of the skills teachers possess is that they are trained to tell stories. They do it all day and may not even recognize when they are telling stories.

While this may not appear obvious to the educator, let us consider. Educators are qualified to teach. They do so by composing a plan. Often as part of that larger "storyboard" there exist smaller messages, like parts of an anthology. An interesting lesson can be learned, a funny experience, a goal achieved; all shared with a teacher's students. These are so ingrained into the fabric of teachers' lessons, that they may not consciously think about it. Yet some of the moments that most captivate their students are those when they share an inspiring, or sad, or triumphant story. Students then are living vicariously through that event, or story.

If sharing a story that engages learners enables them to feel the experience as if it were their own, living the experience along with teachers, we can work this to their advantage. Teachers can access stories to help children heal. That is why story therapy has not only sustained from the ancient philosophers and orators of history but are again gaining in recognition of their benefits. Backed by the science that proves it works (VanDeBrake, 2018), this text offers one more method to aid children, applying the techniques of story therapy.

Stories help listeners alter negative shredding effects of over-thinking and conscious reasoning that our primal brains tend to resort to. Stories tap into the subconscious level of our brains and appeal to our imagination. Therefore, offering story therapy to present mantras of hope, of suggestion by the listener, enables the openness to change for the child. The effect for teachers works because they may not understand how or why, they just need to know it does, and then institute the practice.

Teachers may still fear that they are not equipped to tell a story to effect. Yet if a story does not work right away, there is no permanent damage. The child simply heard an entertaining message, which likely still had the effect of helping other students' engagement, and classroom management. Maybe it helped other kids in the class. At the very least, this is not a harmful technique to try. So how do we try this out?

First, remember that teachers are already storytellers and come armed with the basic tools to tell a story. They typically do not need extensive training on storytelling approaches. Rather, they need to be made aware of how they can message a convincing story, through example and reference of personal or known story themes. Observers and classroom visitors are examples of those who can reinforce this with teachers.

Next, teachers can be guided to find the larger profile of a child's life. Since we know that teachers are most often dealing with some children who are overstressed, taxed, or traumatized, this concept should remain simple and the focus of the story should be organized around themes like hope, inspiration, and productive struggle. Overcoming seemingly impossible obstacles serve as a great catch all. There are many stories centered around this, as evidenced in narrative approaches (Epston, 2013).

Consider telling a story that touches on many or all the senses. This has the effect of hypnotically communicating at the deeper subconscious level. Guide teachers to present descriptive language with sound, sight, taste, and smell. The story does not have to be factual to accomplish this. Inspiring movies, which are based on true events, or adapted from the true life of a figure may influence a child's thinking (such as a great athlete or actress) as well.

Hollywood interjects fiction into the best "based on true events" stories, to generate a more entertaining storyline. Teachers can have fun doing the same as they completely captivate listeners. This has the effect of so deeply connecting the learner, it is not unlike a deep dream state a child can experience. Watch their eyes and body language as they disappear into the storyline, completely immersed.

If teachers remain concerned about their ability, they can share stories from texts, blogs, and other online sources. These are readily available, are presented in the right context, and can aid the listener in deciphering their own experiences. Doing so within this therapeutic context establishes a strong foundation to initiate from for those impacted by the effects of trauma. Bear in mind too, that we are not aiming to "cure" a child of their trauma. Rather, these are powerful, efficient methods to support their road to recovery.

Story therapy is the most common form of language. It is different from common practices; those that do not work at least some of the time. Consider trying something new, something different. The real question is, why wouldn't a teacher try a concept like story therapy, knowing no damage can occur from it? Over time, effectively told stories do work.

## Classroom Context

Whether teachers are incorporating their own accounts into stories, or are borrowing from the classics, or from online resources, they may wonder, "when and in what context should I be engaging in story therapy?" This is like other strategies in this text, simpler than at first glance, and should remain congruent with content delivery and curriculum. Most teachers are expected to follow a sequence but within that framework, have a degree of professional discretion. Obvious contexts, like language arts classrooms provide a natural forum for integrating story.

Other content areas can also be considered; woven into the plan. Social studies offers rich historical perspectives. Science offers storylines including evidence of overcoming the odds, and biographies of inventors and scientists. Physical education and health include athletes and sports teams who offer an inspiring theme, and wellness curriculum. World languages extend to the historical roots of people in those nations where the language is spoken. Even mathematics can be used to demonstrate the progress of an individual, who fought through a challenge, demonstrated with charting of data for how they overcame the odds.

Sharing a story and integrating it with the curriculum should not be a time-consuming process for classroom teachers and students. One cannot spend endless hours each week engaging learners in stories at the cost of meeting overall curricular requirements. This field guide proposes that story therapy does not have to, nor should it be time consuming, or take away from the fidelity of daily instruction for most content area teachers and their students.

Like other concepts introduced in this guide, consider a mini lesson or Do Now/exit type of activity in which a short story is incorporated, not exclusive to serving the needs of a small group of distressed learners. Rather, this can benefit everyone. Like good practices taught by highly effective educators, great teachers use tools for all students, to help those in need and enhance learning for everyone.

In this way, periodic stories associated with the content enable all learners to stand to gain. Remember that students not visibly demonstrating the effects of trauma still likely experience some degree of stress and anxiety at times. These "pep talk" types of stories can and will help them (and you!) as well.

Many can be delivered with an underlying life lesson, such as: we all stand to win.

Powerful short stories can take five minutes or less. They do not always have to connect to the lesson, and teachers may even conceive of a Friday story session or some variation of an exclusive time dedicated to story. Or they can fit into your lesson. The point is teachers have options. These options are theirs to choose from. They are viable and can benefit teacher, class and especially the wellness of children most in need.

## Positive Self-Talk

Reference to case studies and stories of success illustrate how it takes an investment in time and sustained processes to achieve positive outcomes. Getting slightly out of your comfort zone steadily by goal setting is an important exercise in positive outcomes. With support and direction, this can be achieved far more consequentially. Positive self-talk studies have examined methods for applying this technique and the demonstrable success with which results are indicated. Eagleson, Hayes, Matthews, Perman, and Hirsch ( 2016) found that replacing negative thoughts with positive ones reduced anxiety in participants studied.

It should come as no surprise at this point that very little research exists on positive self-talk and its effects on children. As repeatedly indicated in numerous examples of strategies for addressing trauma and anxiety, there is a gap that exists in both research and literature for supporting children. Why? One answer may be the limitations of pursuing research on childhood effects.

Anyone who has engaged in studies involving children can attest to the tremendous obstacles in investigating minors. Institutional Review Boards (IRBs) are structured to carefully audit the ethical oversight of research and are extremely vigilant about limitations to studying children. This creates considerable challenges for examining the effects of trauma among other studies with underage populations.

These restrictions are with good cause; as minors, children must be protected against questionable ethical practices in research. Minors are without the power to consent, and with vulnerabilities that must be protected. However, this does not account for the less formal obligation of general literature publications on anecdotal practices working with children and therefore, this type of information will continue to be offered throughout the text.

Returning to the benefits of positive self-talk: a meta-analysis of studies concluded that self-talk greatly benefits individuals experiencing symptoms of trauma and anxiety. Additionally, findings demonstrated that small shifts in the language people use to refer to themselves during self-reflection substantially impacted their capacity to govern their thoughts, feelings, and behavior during periods of stress. This impacted individuals with anxiety and/or trauma (Kross et al., 2014).

Bearing in mind the benefits of positive and constructive self-talk, a caution should be noted regarding the degree and depth of employing this technique. Positive self-talk, like any effective approach works well, when used correctly. Overuse or lack of authenticity risks projecting an adverse effect. In other words, training students to say, "I deserve to feel good," when they in fact do not does not qualify as an effective method, since they harbor a stronger feeling about how they feel, in reality.

Teaching a vulnerable child to say something such as, "I deserve to learn how to feel better about myself," may gain more authentic buy-in and leaves the child with a growth mindset opportunity shift. This may sound like a small shift but as outlined earlier, subtle shifts, in progressive ways can create a ripple effect. Momentum matters, and it starts small, expanding through these minor shifts, progressing steadily. The same applies to any approach where a constructive repetitious cycle replaces negative thoughts embedded within calculated timelines.

Although length of time in application can help, an overuse can make self-talk feel excessive and unproductive and subsequently, be abandoned by the child. Be certain to have the child reflect when they have an increased likelihood to be in the right state of mind, with a balance of authenticity in their conscious thought exercises, and a productive length of practice. It would be best like all measures for tracking student goals, to monitor this by documenting and have the child apply self-reflection tactics.

Like our focus on small wins, the previous study revealed the power of small shifts, from the scope of self-talk. This rather persuasive argument leads to the determination to reinforce students in the facilitation of developing skills to manage and regulate their self-talk. This will be addressed in the upcoming chapter. On the topic of regulation, a great deal exists in the literature about the value of self-regulation, related to self-talk.

## Self-Regulation as a Tool for Trauma Reduction

There is broad evidence about the positive effects of guided self-regulation practices for a child's development. Self-regulation, like all other strategies outlined in this guide is not one isolated mechanism, nor is there one approach that works best for all. The options for implementation of self-regulation techniques are as complex as the reasons children arrive at the classroom door with adverse effects from trauma.

Therefore, it is of paramount importance to have a catalog of options to tinker with. Getting it right takes time and practice and this investment is well worth it. Learning to apply the right approach, in the right context to elicit the optimal response requires commitment and the execution of exploration. Start small and shift up as the child begins to demonstrate an aptitude for the strategy. Alter or abandon a given strategy if an adverse response appears to emerge. You can always return later at different readiness levels.

Implementing goal setting within the classroom context can serve as an excellent protocol for children to self-regulate and has yielded positive results. In a study of middle school students, teachers taught children about goal-setting, self-reflection, and self-regulation (Patel, Smith, Fitzsimmons, Kara, & Detmer, 2012). Students were guided to set performance goals, giving them an opportunity to excel in areas of focus, by becoming mastery oriented.

Goal setting is well established as a major component in the path leading from trauma to success, as outlined in this text. As a reminder, these goals should not be too lofty, too grandiose, and are best sequenced in a gradual set of steps. Goal setting is a common feature defined in Individualized Education Plans (IEPs) for students classified with special needs.

Children with IEPs who suffer from the effects of trauma benefit from goal setting that addresses their state of distress and subsequently aides in support of their overall success. Yet there are also many children without IEPs who do not receive this same support and they would greatly benefit from a regimented goal setting plan.

Since the primary purpose of this text is to find a viable path to provide for the needs of all students who face the challenges brought on by trauma, enlisting methods congruent with IEPs serve to benefit students from precise and individualized goal setting (IGS). This triggers the necessary script for teachers to navigate through to implement itemized goal setting.

The expectation to create an IGS for every student may seem like a bold and daunting objective to strive for with the typical teacher, already burdened with the many demands of teaching, high stakes testing, and compliances demands. Yet it is critical for schools and their teachers to recognize the need to create the IGS, not only despite their busy, demanding day to day challenge but, because of these challenges.

Teachers must embrace the benefit to provide a foundation for students forged to propel them from, and in the process gain a lifelong skill necessary to succeed beyond the shelter of class-rooms. For students, it will be beneficial then to employ a method for individualizing student support through an individualized learning plan, a coordinated plan that will be discussed in the next chapter.

## Chapter Summary

Equipped with the tools to help assess and track students to ensure we are ready to offer them the necessary tools, it is time to help them engage in the motivational drive toward small wins. Small wins are very well discussed in the literature, yet little is covered regarding this serving to aid children, especially those who are recovering from that distress.

Helping students to experience this and to understand its value helps them gain a sense of control, something referred to as their internal locus of control.

Internal locus of control allows students to recognize the important distinction between a growth and fixed mindset. Accepting that they as individuals can remain on a path of being able to eventually reach for an achievement, rather than being stuck in a mindset of not being able to allow for a liberation from a restrictive outlook helps them push forward toward an open mindset to grow and develop toward that achievement.

Positive behavior support techniques like the positive to negative ratio work to help students see the small wins psychology more clearly.

Charting small wins helps the learner to see their progress more literally. Be thoughtful in how you illustrate this since there will be setbacks. The importance is to see the overall upward trend.

Distanced self-talk allows individuals to separate the problem from themselves in a constructive way.

Post-traumatic growth is evidenced in history as something that can be accomplished, and this can be applied to students struggling with post-traumatic stress.

Story therapy can be provided by teachers, who by nature of their training and experience are natural story tellers. Story can immerse students in ways that make them feel as if they are living the experience, and we can use this to leverage our ability to aid them in their road to recovery.

Positive self-talk has been shown to help individuals work through their struggles and to benefit from getting out of their comfort zone.

Self-regulation skill development helps vulnerable students to strengthen their management of feelings and conduct to solidify their response to trauma.

Individualized goal setting is an important part of targeting student specific methods for helping them grow.

# 8

# Instituting an Individualized Plan in Collaboration With Student(s)

Individualized learning plans (ILPs) are attracting attention as instruments for students to benefit from, with a more personalized approach to their learning. ILPs can be instrumental in helping to form the foundation of a child's learning trajectory. This customized format empowers the learner to join with a team to work toward their tailored goals. Their team is typically composed of teachers, a counselor, parents and most importantly, themselves. Many of the methods recommended within this text can and certainly should be incorporated into the framework of an ILP.

It is understandable that those in the education field may first mistake the term ILP for IEP. An IEP is a more commonly known formally implemented support document for students with special needs, as an Individualized Education Plan (IEP). This is a legally binding support document that ensures the child with learning, physical, or behavioral challenges receives the modifications necessary for them to perform in the least

DOI: 10.4324/9781003162971-8

restrictive environment possible, and with modifications to aid in their learning.

Yet children with challenges that have an IEP represent only one-seventh (14%) of the student population in the United States. Many students who are not classified with an IEP and fall within the other 86% experience distress and trauma and would greatly benefit from a plan, tailored to their individual goals. One could argue that every child would benefit from a plan tailored to their individual goals toward meeting success.

ILPs should not be exhaustive documents that require considerable labor to construct and subsequently monitor. In fact, they should not be extensive, instead serving as a dynamically simplistic plan that can adapt with the child, both through time and milestones achieved, as well as to equip them as they encounter potential setbacks. ILPs should be concise, while remaining inclusive of child-specific goals. Below in Figure 8.1 is one illustration of a model for an ILP document, offered as a template for use:

| ILP Template: | |
| --- | --- |
| Student name: | Date of birth: |
| Grade: | |

**Review of progress will be based on collection and analysis of data**

- formal classroom and broader assessment data include data from formative assessments, including collection of Do Now, exit card, and form prompt responses
- feedback from the student
- feedback from the parents/guardians

*All decisions regarding student learning should be based on a scope of data sources. Individual Learning Plans serve to personalize the teaching and learning program, support improvement in identified areas and will be monitored and edited regularly, because it serves as a living document.*

**FIGURE 8.1** ILP Template

| Learning improvement goals | Learning outcomes |
|---|---|
| Priority areas for improvement. Consider: <br>• engagement<br>• attendance<br>• behavior | List relevant learning outcomes linked to the learning improvement goals.<br><br>Consider:<br>• engagement<br>• attendance<br>• behavior |
| **School and classroom strategies revised pedagogy**<br><br>Consider:<br>• prompts and charting of progress<br>• classroom learning interventions<br>• small group/individual support<br>• academic or behavior expectations | **Parents/ guardians – expectations/ support**<br><br>Identify in partnership:<br>• expectations of parents/guardians<br>• level of support that can be provided by parents/guardians<br>• how the school can support parents/caregivers |
| **Processes for collection of data**<br><br>Identify:<br>• data collection methods<br>• how progress will be measured<br><br>**Timeline for review and revision of plan**<br><br>Individual learning plans should be measured and revised regularly, towards the mission of a trajectory goal sequence (small wins). | |

**FIGURE 8.1** (Continued)

The main principles of this document place emphasis on small, informal data sources that are tracked and monitored over time and organized within the child's personalized plan. Everything within the living ILP culminates in a review and revision cycle that embodies the practices outlined in this text, and that engage relevant participants who are involved in representing the child's team.

Involved parties serve on the student's education team, as previously noted. Consider also dynamic structures of your school community that allow for other supportive participants.

For instance, you may find it beneficial to include a mentor where a mentoring program exists, a coach or band director, and anyone else associated with the child's program of study.

Schools may elect to use a standardized form like the one in Figure 8.1 or create their own. It is recommended that a generic template provide the capacity to be amended within the unique community and student populations goals/vision it is being incorporated with. Consider the values, visions and goals of your community and do not get stuck on a regimen that may not be applicable. Remember that everything in this book is and should be adaptable to a best fit, is not commercially based and restrictive and should instead serve as a field guide, not as a finite structure.

Avoid a complicated array of dozens of templates which would make the conciseness of the product hard to track due to the complexity of the variations. Be mindful of some common formats that contain widely acceptable and positive goal statements, and always consider a trajectory that can be charted, adapted, and serve as a best fit for the child.

Regarding the course layout, this is where tracking data in small data sets over time is a factor. Having a framework to develop a tracking mechanism, one that is not complicated is necessary. A path for the child can be developed such as in the skill sets embodied in one school's language arts program, where mastery of linear sequence literacy is carefully scripted, something called a *confer menu* (*Reading Workshop*, n.d.). You can find these, in alphanumeric order. The earlier part of the alphabet (A-B-C) represents introductory reading skills, and later parts of the alphabet represent students further along with their literacy skills.

Within this type of guide, teachers working with learners measure their progress through formative reading measures, to determine their level of proficiency. The formative measures are instructionally designed around conferencing, a method of instruction that facilitates discussion focused on topics within the literacy skill components laid out in the confer menu (*Reading Workshop*, n.d.). These are structured to instructional content. Like all curricular learning experiences, teachers can gain a great deal of information from their learners through conferencing on topics they are learning about.

Student responses to a reading prompt can tell us a great deal about a child's values, concerns, challenges, and beliefs. Often, referral to a school counselor may result from a writing excerpt composed by a student in response to a reading, where they make a comparison to a troubled child within the text and draw parallels as to how they may align to symptoms from the impact of trauma.

Content area subjects offer milestones for student achievement and taking students through the sequence in a transparent way that is shared with them helps learners to see those sequences and their successes resulting from each. This is another example of the benefits of celebrating small wins and illustrating for learners their demonstrated progression. It is something they may not otherwise see or realize without documenting their progress in this manner.

Frameworks like the confer menu (*Reading Workshop*, n.d.) are present everywhere in school curriculum guides. All content areas have some sequence of content schemas. The problem is that their sophistication is often beyond the practical application of measurement on a single day's data set, or shorter sets of linear steps. Breaking these down into component parts like the confer menu (*Reading Workshop*, n.d.) allows for measurement of micro skill sets. More significant, this makes a practical and tangible progression something students can visualize as they are tracked.

While this text does not propose to rewrite curriculum, and since the goal is to simplify this process and stack effective methods anyway, use your existing plan and simplify it. This is a major factor for students seeing and experiencing their small wins. Consider clarifying a day's task with student friendly objectives, or essential questions. Be sure to have students own these as their goals, not the teachers, or anyone else. ILPs can become part of a child's digital portfolio, in that it can serve as a form of a table of contents for the files associated with their continuous tracking within the portfolio.

## Digital Portfolio Tracking

The essence of a comprehensive warehouse for tracking student artifacts over time should include:

1. The capacity to store all kinds of files. These include documents, presentations, data sheets, audio, and video files.
2. Free or inexpensive resources.
3. Reliable sources that sustain beyond shifts to a premium cost or drastic change at an unknown later date.
4. Being easily monitored and used by the student, and the members of his ILP, and of the teachers who cycle through their years of education.

Therefore, consider one of several parallel options, mainly within the resilience apparent on Google or Microsoft domains. While there is not, nor should there be a preference for either of these or any other resources, they are among the most stable cloud-based storage systems and remain free or inexpensive components of a larger network within school systems.

As big players in the global market and vested in supporting education through a broader business model, stick with one of these, Microsoft or Google, unless your district is confined to a pre-existing cloud-based system that they have invested in.

These systems are easily shareable across teacher, parents, and students. They should be accessed from year to year as students transition grades and teachers. This is perhaps one of the biggest gaps in connecting student progress in a child's progression from one year to the next. Implementing portfolio use marks an opportunity in our monitoring of student wellness. Additionally, as part of a broader system to monitor student progress and wellness, these became even more valuable.

Student portfolios maintained over time are excellent resources for later college entry, trade school or professional reference. Essentially, these may serve as living, longitudinal resumes. They can be referred to by a counselor assigned to work with college and career admissions, and more. They are robust resources that should be developed with some sense of order. Keep in mind some degree of consistency for organizing of student products.

Examples of student work can include some of the following:

◆ A table of contents organizing the components with links to each item (the ILP should be part of this).
◆ A list of term definitions that will help make the portfolio interpretable.
◆ Individualized learning plans, with revised versions, tracked regularly, quarterly, by semester and annually.
◆ Visuals, charts (including some of progress), images, audio, video and other items.
◆ Performance based assessment scores.
◆ Reading logs.
◆ Images of students working.
◆ Anecdotal notes from one-on-one or small group time with students (e.g., guided reading notes).
◆ Video recordings of readings or performances (for ePortfolios).
◆ A sample paragraph of writing featuring a few key writing techniques.
◆ Sample writing compositions produced by the student including journal entries stories, poems, songs, and scripts.

- ◆ An inventory of graded math assessments, illustrating performance trends.
- ◆ Student work from fine arts classes such as Art and Music.

Portfolios may sound like a major undertaking to form in gathering this compilation of content, a plethora that makes it challenging to decipher or review. It may seem that this would concern even big data proponents. Yet, remember that this is where the ILP comes into play. The ILP should be designed to harness the information hosted within the portfolio, which best serves to inform everyone involved, regarding a student's progress.

The ILP provides the capacity to map for educators what the focus is on regarding student progress, and offers an adaptable approach for modification, at appropriate intervals. This alone should strengthen the value of the ILP, as it sustains in the form of a living document for a child, one who may be impacted by effects of trauma. Being equipped with this profile offers educators the tools presented within this resource guide to help learners move beyond their distress.

## Student Friendly Objectives

When an observer entered a classroom to visit one day, he leaned over after a few minutes to check in with a student. He wanted to gauge the student's familiarity with the lesson objective; to determine if students in his walk-throughs that day were clear on the learning goals. Listed on the board was the acronym, SWBAT (*students will be able to*), alongside the objective. The supervisor whispered in the student's ear, "can you tell me what your goal is for today?" The student looked up and replied in a non-whisper, "I don't know, we just have to Swab it!" The whole class turned to this corner of the room, drawn to the interaction.

While this story provides some comic relief, it signifies a broader issue. Clearly, this student did not understand what

SWBAT meant, and worse, it was even more unlikely he understood what his goal was for the lesson, considering his response. Student-friendly objectives are best crafted, or at least translated, by students themselves. Educators feeling rushed to get through a lesson may find time a factor that is difficult to invest in for characterizing the objective. However, laying this foundation leads to greater understanding, empowerment, and student success.

Student-friendly objectives, or student learning targets as they are also referred to, are presented visually and auditorily to learners as a path toward ensuring students know the purpose of the lesson. Taking this a step further, students benefit by owning their learning goal. This occurs when a brief discussion about the learning goal engages them in constructive dialogue about its meaning. Therefore, having students state the objective, and then asking others to describe its purpose are concrete ways to accomplish this.

In addition to clarifying the learning target, student empowerment can be a factor of taking the time to invest in this process. Therefore, introducing the objective at the beginning is only a part of the process. Checking to determine whether the goal was achieved at the end of the lesson, and having students remind each other what the goal is as they work are also factors in helping them understand their ongoing goals.

By engaging learners in this check, teachers are encouraging continuous assessment. Students can better internalize the end game, and how this impacts their overall learning experience. Learning connections are an important component in the child's overall comfort level with the learning.

A way to accomplish mid-lesson checks is for the teacher to call for a reminder, prompting students to consider, what is our goal? What are you looking to achieve? Setting this up with triggers for learners is an effective midpoint check-in. For instance, projecting this on screen, and calling students attention to the learning target provides the advantage of reinforcing the objective, and empowering learners to persevere in attaining the goal.

At the close of a lesson, calling for students to address whether they met the lesson objective may be accomplished in a variety of ways. Exit cards are often employed by teachers, and they can be used to collect data for tracking purposes, as previously highlighted. There is value in checking exit responses before students depart to the next class.

Calling on one or two students to respond to exit checks allows for a confirmation of understanding and may elicit a recognition from the teacher that more emphasis on the content or an adaptation of the lesson is warranted. Additionally, student sharing of exit responses adds to the empowerment students experience as they remain connected to their own learning. Additionally, having students share their understanding often helps translate to other learners who may not interpret the teacher's efforts to convey this same learning principle.

Implications related to student ILPs increase the value of their participation, while sustaining engagement of learners. Next, we will look at how to construct a student-friendly objective, for the purpose of making clear the goals and determining student understanding.

## How to Write a Student Friendly Objective/ Learning Targets

Step one: Identify the nouns – these are the key words students need to know or understand. Underline these.

Step two: Identify the verbs –

Example, identify, analyze, infer – these are the skills students need to be able perform. Circle these.

Step three: Identify what students need to learn to master the learning outcome

Example, identify the front, back and title page of a text. Note these.

i. Vocabulary – title
ii. Parts of a book

   a) Title page
   b) Front cover
   c) Back cover

Step four: Describe the outcome/success criteria – the student will be able to . . .

Learning Outcomes in SFO language: I will define the title, determine the title page, front cover, and back cover of a book. I know I have been successful when I can discuss the contents of each of these.

Finally, student friendly objectives should contain the elements of a SMART goal, if they are to be clear, goal orientated and have an outcome:

Specific well defined to students; observable to teachers; answers a wh-question (who, what, when, where, why, how)
Measurable Can be evaluated; able to determine if objective is either reached, or not
Achievable The objective is rigorous enough to challenge students, yet they are academically, emotionally, and mentally ready for the objective
Time Bound set a time limit for the objective to be accomplished – not a fixed time frame, but a range like one to two class periods (in case your exit activity determines a need to further reinforce).

Here is an example of taking a difficult to decipher teacher objective and clarifying it as a more student friendly version. Sample comparisons between SWBAT and SFO:

SWBAT language: *SWBAT synthesize a rationale for the downfall of Rome.*

SFO language: *Today, I will be able to categorize reasons for the fall of Rome. I know I've got it when I can explain/justify/prove the causes for the fall of Rome.*

Essential Questions were discussed previously, to generate responses from learners operating for the purpose of data collection. Essential questions make clear what the pursuit of the activity is, and prioritizes a plan, or objective for learners. Framing with essential questions can serve similar benefits as student-friendly objectives in considering student responses that demonstrate understanding. They also serve the purpose of streamlining what the goals are for their learning. Next, we will explore the benefits of physical structure that support learners in distress.

## Flexible Seating

One of the most intriguing outcomes from virtual learning that took place during the quarantine period of 2020 was that children were not seated traditionally in a classroom, in a controlled setting where seating arrangements are mostly arranged by educators. Teachers reported at times humorous and at other times worrisome circumstances, as they virtually entered the homes of their students. Descriptions of children hanging upside down off their bed, or of siblings racing by half dressed, darting across the screen created some of those unusual moments.

When it comes to outcomes for students, the greatest educators consistently and skillfully see beyond status quo. They understand that the outcome, the end goal is far more important than a telegraphed set of instructions to follow for completing a task. In one school, teachers who were exceptional, were highly effective in their work and encouraged children to produce, did not demand they sit in a precisely ordered manner. Granted, they discussed digital ethics and appropriateness of responses among other important student-citizenship topics. Yet they balanced understanding of limits with student willingness from across this digital spectrum.

Right-sized, or flexible seating was a concept that took hold several years prior to the pandemic. Covid-19 forced educators' hands to see with concrete evidence that the allowances provided to learners during digital instruction gave students the latitude necessary to learn in their environment. It further allowed students to be motivated, be taught in their natural space, and to feel as though they have some say in how they could learn. These factors are not only a good idea for effective instruction within schools; they are essential in gaining the attention of at risk, distressed and traumatized learners.

In addition, to offering choice, students benefit from many other components when presented with flexible seating options. Following is a summary of numerous additional advantages.

1. Physical management – be sure to encourage students to move. They are not built to sit, for hours every day, staring into a computer screen, or at a smartboard. In addition to urging them to get up and stretch from time to time, encourage comfort – think about your wobblers and rockers. They are self-managing and that helps them learn (so long as this does not pose a distraction to others).

2. Comfort – one educator recalls sitting in a row as a student, not permitted to move and getting in trouble, all the time for his restlessness. He figured out that he could take a pencil and swing it between his thumb and forefinger, back and forth, just to remain comfortable. It did not make noise and released pent up energy. What if he had not figured this out? Allow students comfort, so they have choice in releasing their pent-up energy. In addition to letting them move, let them sit in their comfort zone, as long as they are learning.

3. Community and collaboration – less personalized, more mechanized standard seating arrangements depersonalize

our collective ability to bond, to connect to one another. Think about some of the greatest philosophers. When they taught, they gathered students in a circle, at the same eye level and they sat together. Provide allowance for this kind of community experience. Additionally, the less formal set up of flexible seating promotes a more interactive, engaging coffee shop ambience to encourage interactions.

4. Engagement is increased – creating more student control and less teacher-centric placement motivates student engagement. Physical comfort allows learners to gain a sense of interest in setting the stage by sitting or standing in a manner that is conducive to their learning style. Additionally, students entering a classroom at the onset which offers welcoming signs of comfort and choice reduce tension and help many students with distress in their life.

5. Sensory Input – flexible seating has the advantage of stimulating students' tactile senses. The sense of touch can help children focus and process information. Sensory input is especially beneficial for students with focusing challenges, something many children under duress experience, and exhibit.

Communicate expectations clearly when arranging right-sized seating. *Caution*: you cannot just announce that your room is now a flexible seating environment. Like any good management technique when offering students choice and independence, clearly establish why you are providing this option and outline some new classroom management expectations. This includes developing a system to make seating choice fair and nondisruptive. The advantage of this proactive plan is that students generally respond very well to fairness and equity. Use this to your advantage and explore scenarios where all kids experience the opportunity of choice.

Helping students to determine their own best practices in seating comfort also requires processing of higher-order thinking skills, like problem-solving, and emotional adeptness, such as conflict resolution. There is value in fostering turn-taking and patience, work-life skills that serve to benefit children. The communication skills necessary to reinforce this adds to the benefit of learners impacted by trauma who are learning to work out day to day challenges.

## Chapter Summary

Individual learning plans (ILPs) are personalized supportive documents that remain dynamic and allow for student participation as we track and monitor their progress, using tactics characterized in previous chapters.

Alongside a child's ILP are the application of digital portfolios, which can track a student along their academic continuum, so that one year is connected to the next, even as the student receives new teachers year to year.

Student friendly objectives – helping students understand the objective in clear age relevant terms helps them gain ownership in their capacity to seek out and accomplish the goal, empowering them for doing so.

Flexible seating allows students under distress to find ways to self-compensate, and to gain a sense of control over their learning environment.

# 9

# Considerations for Educators' Management of Their Trauma – How to Grow as Models for Learners

This text is dedicated to student wellness and achievement. The path to greater success for children lies in fostering specific and targeted strategies, over time that are powerful change agents. Ultimately, students can learn skills of independence that allow them to activate their self-regulation skills and nourish their own wellness. Teachers are offered a proposition in this text, a practical approach. If teachers are to be successful with implementing these techniques, they need to take care of themselves first, before they can lend a well-placed hand.

The importance of teacher self-care has attracted recent attention, as educators endure the day-to-day increased demands and challenges of high stakes expectations, alongside a population that is changing in demand and need. Children are arriving at classroom doors with ever increasing and wide-ranging concerns. This is hard work, it is emotionally invested, and it is draining. Students come with challenges beyond teacher

DOI: 10.4324/9781003162971-9

training, including trauma. Supporting teachers must be prioritized to help them address their students many and varied challenges. By helping to support those in the trenches helping children, schools can accomplish helping both.

The need to provide tangible examples that faculty can learn about today and use tomorrow to support children was presented. This is as important for educators, under the duress of day-to-day and newer challenges, like a pandemic that completely reconfigured how they taught and practiced their profession. It cannot go understated that teaching and learning was turned on its side for an extended period. The pressure associated with this only perpetuated pre-existing stress and anxiety teachers faced with already demanding expectations.

Establishing that teachers face tremendous stressors which can and have triggered trauma in their own professional and personal lives, educational leaders, professional development coordinators, and staff developers should support teachers' wellness, alongside their lifelong learning experiences. If teachers are to help children who endure trauma, stress anxiety, even a combination of these, they must be provided the tools to do so.

So, what can be done to help already stressed out, even traumatized educators, find their own safe space? Before we can answer that, understand with certainty that educators must first take care of themselves before they can help their students. This should be viewed as a definitive assertion. Take care of your teachers, so they can take care of your students. The two cannot be separated. They are directly linked.

Like the three-step process for supporting and helping traumatized learners excel, outlined here is a path of self-care and wellness that follows a similar step-by-step sequence. What is different however, is that the components are laid out to operate in a self-guided format. As adults, teachers are professionals who have developed some capacity to manage their own lives and self-care is part of that capacity. They just need a roadmap.

Consider using this chapter as a guide for school communities to assist teachers with.

The three parts of teacher care protocols are woven throughout and include:

1. Identifying the problem for educators.
2. Offering a menu of quick, easy to use tools and techniques to solve the problem. Remember these are best utilized in a "stacked" manner, with moving parts crisscrossing to compound the effect for the recipient.
3. Moving beyond maintenance, find the best version of you.

## The Problem and Techniques to Overcome

At the core of their work and purpose, educators teach because they care about helping others. To fully function, we must acknowledge both the extraordinary responsibility teachers own, and provide the structures to do so with a focus on self-care. This matters now more than ever, as we adapt to a new normal, following a once in a lifetime pandemic, a recognition of national equity issues and escalating stressors associated with social media misinformation.

Social media misinformation persists all around us. This disinformation is confusing, stressful, and unhealthy. Harmful to us, and by proxy, those we teach, we also have a fundamental responsibility to model for impressionable children how to manage all the confusing information surrounding us. Armed with a device that has far greater sophistication then what landed humans on the moon, we are bombarded, with not enough time to decipher it all, and much of it is inaccurate and powerfully deceptive.

There is evidence all around us about the strong association between significant social media use and increased danger for depression, anxiety, and loneliness. Yet we all remain so grossly connected, all the time because we need to be, right? Consider that at one school during the pandemic quarantine, a principal saw the effects of her faculty struggling with the signs of stress, anxiety, and trauma. They were tired, bleary eyed, confused, scared, and all the while had to calm the nerves of anxious students and parents. This seemed daunting. The principal decided to try something different, to challenge her faculty with an incentive, one that seemed well worth it.

## The Weekend Challenge

The principal was as guilty as anyone. She was tethered to her phone, frequently checking the alarming number of messages and updates coming through at unpredictable moments. She felt compelled to always be "on." After all, what if she missed something? There were the dopamine hits, as each message triggered her, pinging her phone. Her cousin's latest update, or the radical onslaught of another misinformation campaign. How could she remove herself? By modeling the way. But wouldn't that be impossible? She had to try something.

The principal announced to her faculty that she recognized their challenges and proposed that they all take a *Weekend Challenge*. Just pick one day, only one from the two-day weekend to stay off computers, phones, tablets, email, social media, everything. Put your smartwatch away too. Remove all alerts that constantly bombard your attention. If you do this, submit a form on Monday morning that professes you met the *Weekend Challenge*.

Following this was a lottery in which all faculty who entered could win. What they could win did not matter. The point was, do this together. Like those challenging each other in a fitness class goal, this was a bonding experience that brought the faculty back together from the digital divide, by being *disconnected*! Disconnection sounded unfamiliar like unknown territory.

What happened next? The faculty expressed a tremendous sense of inspiration, due to this liberation, as they were more in touch with their family members. For that one day, they took a walk back in time. Newsflash: nothing tragic happened by remaining off their devices. The world did not stop while being offline. In fact, their responses were quite different than expected.

It was no coincidence that when asked how this experience made faculty feel, there were remarkably consistent results. Had it been more stressful knowing you might miss something, or were you in some way better off? Over and over, results revealed that every experience not involving screen time was connected to more pleasure and contented enjoyment. Contrastingly, on the other day of the weekend, every screen related event was linked to less fulfillment.

The principal continues these challenges, much to the joy of her faculty who continue to feel reconnected and reminded of the value of going offline, ironically through this communal networking effect She also professed to her faculty that her family noticed how she was more *connected* to them when she removed the vices of digital bonds. She modeled the way, and her faculty became healthier for it.

This simple technique may seem obvious, but we can become quickly clouded by the digital world. One example is the sad reality online that perpetuates the game of telephone – a true anxiety inducing trigger for those familiar with this current global anomaly. Let us consider one story, shared by another administrator who faced the consequences of social media gone bad.

A shocking falsehood was gossiped about on Facebook about a student who had brought guns to school and how this child placed the members of this school community in grave, life-threatening danger. According to the story, the child was carted off to juvenile detention after a conflict. The truth: a student had brought a letter opener to school, and when confronted by a peer, confessed openly, reporting to the office, on his own, though he had no ill intent.

The blunder many school representatives make in scenarios like this one is to simply ignore the absurd social media misrepresentation that perpetuates, or decide to send a communication to families, offering an ambiguous response in a feeble attempt to correct the misinformation campaign. This only increases the angst of well-meaning but misinformed community members and suddenly, everyone is involved, possibly even the media! Here is why this approach is futile:

◆ Clarifying misinformation via transparency comforts worried parents surrounded by inaccuracies. This straightforward approach builds trust in a school community, calming the nerves of everyone.
◆ If wisely responded to, school communities can effectively shift the narrative to a positive one. That is healthy for everyone!

This can be accomplished rapidly and save costly time and energy while not having to explain in public at a board meeting or worse to the story hungry media. The simple answer is to engage families who personally depend on and request information from the school. It is common for a few sincere well-intentioned individuals to reach out directly to the leadership. That is invaluable and works to the school's advantage, so it should be embraced and leveraged.

Every administrator knows this person or group of persons. Use this to the school's advantage. Do not go on social media and engage. That is where the online game of telephone stubbornly permeates and dangerously evolves. No educational leader should engage there, for their own wellness (first) and for the betterment of their community (second).

Equipped with parents as your resource to shift the narrative, convey a message to them: feel free to post that they have heard directly from you, and that you requested they share a very simple, factual statement in the thread. This could look something like:

I heard directly from (person clarifying), and he/she clarified that the allegations are wrong. He/she noted that a child brought in a letter opener and never showed it to anyone. The letter opener promptly was secured by school officials and the child was issued appropriate disciplinary action. No child was in danger at any time. Please feel free to copy and paste this entire set of facts into your post.

In the circumstance illustrated, the online interchange instantly shifted direction. The school official became the recipient of praise for transparency and for eliminating falsehoods that had come to life due to the online game of telephone. Responses included, "finally, some honest effort at putting parents' minds at ease!" and "wow, straight from the horse's mouth, now I can go back to work resting easy that my child is safe!"

The original fabrication instantly evaporated, and families conveyed relief, effectively and peacefully moving on with their lives. There was no board meeting with a gang of anxious parents, no news media incorrectly diagnosing the story and the school proceeded with its more important day to day operations, helping address real student problems, rather than being distracted by fictional accounts. The principal who made this all happen reported feeling a tremendous amount of faith in a just truth, and a liberation from the very stressors underscored by the social media misinformation that persists on online social media platforms.

## Social Media Makes US Less Intelligent

Overexposure to social media, has profound effects because it distracts us away from the much greater satisfaction of deep work. An invasion of our focus and productivity from the incessant pings and alerts that pull our attention away, makes people highly distractible, agitated, and unsatisfied with their work. This literally has the reverse effect of productive focus we strive for. It is no wonder that adults and children alike are struggling with the triggers that lead to trauma. More will be discussed about deep focus and its connection to overall wellness.

Feelings of social exclusion can arouse physical and psychological damage that results in reduced levels of cognitive thought. Our mind's self-management system takes on the task of regulating a host of feelings triggered by social media, and that process demands cognitive resources that work to inhibit intelligent thinking. Naturally, this results in productivity declines, as decision making becomes reduced (Gambini, 2018). Comparison is a major factor in creating cognitively unhealthy feelings. Remedies to address this among other productivity and wellness inhibitors are presented here and more are offered in the upcoming section.

## Music Therapy

Music is all around us and anyone who has pulled up to a stop light in their car belting out a favorite tune can truly appreciate the immediate impact tuning into our favorite songs and tuning out from the outside stressors stimulates. Different kinds of music and melodies have varying effects on our mindset. Music therapy, like many of the strategies suggested throughout this text, is not new. To reinforce, combining music therapy with other methods, and strategy is the best approach to tip the balance in the right direction for one's personal wellness.

Melody variances impacts our physical and mental wellbeing. Consider an upbeat song that gets your senses primed, invigorating your motivation and energy. This is a helpful approach to prepare for a competitively oriented activity. Yet this would not make sense when you need to sit down and focus on an exam, or to craft a thoughtful linguistic response. In fact, listening to upbeat, fast-paced music may increase aggression triggers and anyone who has written an email they later regret after hitting send knows why. We need to be thoughtful in crafting messages. The right kind of music can impact how this is conveyed.

So, what kind of music, how and when should we be listening to it for the best payoff? This can be considered now in the context of our modern-day access. Armed with our devices as instruments, we can engage in something as private and important as music therapy, with portable access, remotely from wherever we are.

One educator recalls parking in the school lot, as he listened to his favorite music at full blast volume (alternative rock) and seeing the surprised looks of parents and faculty walking across the parking lot, realizing where the music was erupting from! He quickly realized these private moments needed to be stored somewhere, as importantly as they were therapeutic to get him motivated. He now uses earbuds.

The kind of music we listen to can alter how our brain responds. With a focus on anxiety, stress, and depression reducing melodies, consider that when we are in a melancholy state of mind, or things just do not seem to be going well, even the most upbeat music can be slow to reverse our mindset and may ultimately result in failure. Furthermore, we have already established that it can have the reverse effect, even provoking aggressiveness.

Calming techniques include hearing songs that are slower paced, and softer, with a melody that helps put our minds at ease. Think of spa music, classical and even the compelling evidence of a song constructed by sound specialists, specifically designed to target the brain in a way that is evidenced to reduce anxiety. Indeed, there is science to back this claim up.

A study confirmed that a nearly two thirds reduction in participants' overall anxiety occurred when listening to the song *Weightless* (Curtin, n.d.). The band Marconi Union worked alongside sound specialists to craft the perfect balance. The song is eight minutes in length and researchers report a change in mindset after listening for five undisturbed minutes.

The five-minute marker matters. If we can make efficient and powerful adjustments to our own wellness, we need to be able to provide practitioners with practical, moment's notice tactics to quickly engage in with simple access and action. Excusing yourself from the context of your frenzied day, challenged with demands for lengthy periods of time to center yourself is not viable or sustainable. Instead, like most methods presented in this chapter, practitioners can engage in them quickly, and over a short period of time, with significant impact.

The music experience is a very personal one for each of us, so offering preferences dictated by our individual desires is not within the scope of this guide. Educators are encouraged to go with what works best for them. You likely already have favorites that, thinking consciously about, makes sense to keep on hand, in your phone to plug in at a moment's notice with your eyes closed, leaning back in your chair, or wherever else you may find solace. You can quickly find an abundance of choices for free, online by searching *anxiety reducing music*.

## The Satisfaction of Deep Work and Why It Puts Your Mind at Ease

Since work that is focused and uninterrupted is quite literally the opposite of distraction and the scattershot surface work that overtakes our focus, this quality of work has the impact of producing the reverse effect. Unfocused, disorganized, shallow work is rushed, distracted, and deeply unsatisfying. Given the distraction and intensity all around us, with digital alerts, social media misinformation confusing us and agitation arising from it all, it is no wonder we are in an ongoing state of distress.

This is not beneficial to our well-being and missing from all of this is the need to literally *check out* with deep work. Due to the creativity that deep work triggers, and the productivity associated with it, a highly satisfying awareness and therefore, direct remedy to the previously discussed mental and physical distress is activated. In fact, the sense of self improves with the fulfillment and affirmation that deep work has initiated a higher cognitive mindset of creativity and produced a decidedly qualitative production of our work.

Therefore, a feeling of contentment during deep work is provoked. Additionally, this improved sense of self can last far beyond the effects experienced during and immediately after the practice of deep work – days beyond, resulting in positive residual effects. The problem is that making a decision to establish the conditions for deep work require a conscious effort to remove the constant causes of disruptions. We feel compelled to always be *on* and responsive. That is where deep work attempts are interfered with and inhibited.

Having established the critical importance of deep work for our wellbeing, and acknowledging the challenges to provide the means for it, how do we foster the mechanisms to allow for extended, undisrupted conditions? Unlike previous methodologies, this one requires time and a concerted commitment to ascertain. It is well worth the investment. Deep work is so critical to lifelong serenity and well-being that it should be practiced both within and outside of our professional lives.

Remember that if you are unable to access any of the proposed techniques due to a constraint, or a lack of feasibility, there is an inventory of other tools you can choose from. Deep work may even be something that you cannot access in the here and now, but later, over summer vacation or some other, more leisurely and less-time constrained period. There is value in providing educators with the methods in which they can tap into their own deep work, when they are ready.

## Launching Into Deep Focus and Work – Steps to Get There

Reduce TV. Many previously mentioned approaches foster deep work. In addition to separating yourself from the killer of all deep work, digital connectedness and social media, television is another void that while we may consider it to be relaxing, also has the effect of literally dumbing down our senses. Subsequently, this effects our focus, in most circumstances. Let us consider why.

Most programs on TV serve purely entertainment purposes, and this frequently taps our primal senses, not those which draw on the viewer transcending to deeper thought processes. Examples of models of media that may help arouse deeper thought are those that are lesson based, science backed, historical, or other educationally themed topics. It is not suggested that you completely abandon your vegetative moments in front of the TV. Rather, reduce this time, minimize it, and at least be conscious of its effects.

<u>Schedule time for deep work</u>. Arranging for deep work may sound a bit orchestrated but this is an effective way to increase the opportunity for entering the right mindset. Set up your surroundings, so that you have framed an ideal setting to enter focused work. As previously mentioned, establish conditions with music therapy, and other sources for a temporary reprieve from shallow, distracted work, and digital disruptions.

<u>Step into boredom</u> (not a typo!). For those of us who recall long summer days and Saturdays with minimal supervision, think about those drawn out, mundane hot summer days as a child when you spent hours doing seemingly nothing. You may have laid in a field, under a tree, sat in a treehouse, or just stared into space. This might sound counterintuitive: how can the lack of production from standing still stimulate greater creativity and focus?

The absence of distractors can in fact arouse an urge to be stimulated, and this can provoke creativity. Our brains are always searching for meaning and information. This is a major attribute of being human. Curiosity is what drove the evolution of our species far beyond any other in the evolution of the world around us. Our human quest to search for meaning is driven by hunger, and an insatiable desire to gain new information.

That is in why we are so hooked to distractors. They keep our mind occupied and our senses attended to. Deprivation generates in us a hunger that makes us long for enlightenment. Stripping away the distractors that feed our information hungry minds propels us into a higher state of curiosity and desire for thought provocation. This is where critical, higher order thinking kicks in. It requires patience and time, not recommended as a quick fix. Think of a long car ride, or time alone to capture this deep focus prompting boredom. Turn off the car radio and rediscover the liberation of boredom.

## When You Move the Body, You Move the Mind

Many of us have experienced talking on the telephone when we were so deeply engrossed in the conversation with an old friend, or in an intense discussion about an innovative concept with a trusted colleague. If you were walking around your house, or neighborhood, you know the feeling of being stimulated and if you had a step counter, might be startled by how quickly your step count jumped as you paced back and forth, immersed in the discussion. You did not even realize how much you had paced.

What was happening here? How was this possible, and in a way that you were unaware of how active you were? It was as if you were unconscious, completely unaware of your surroundings while you were moving about. The evidence is telling on movement, and how it helps to enlighten our senses and cognition in ways that being sedentary, and stationary cannot. Moving around requires you to get blood circulating throughout your body, so that you can maintain steady movement. In doing so, blood increases everywhere and an increased supply circulating to the brain floods our cognitive senses, too.

Just like the muscles in your body, when blood supply is increased to your brain, you can exert greater force, energy and thought processes. This would seem simple enough but too often the cognitive benefits of movement are overlooked. More mainstream recognition regarding this has taken off recently but slowly, as some individuals have replaced their inactive, seated desks with standing and even with moving treadmill workstations. Flexible seating which was discussed earlier is a mechanism for students to get up and moving during learning as well.

This is not nearly commonplace enough, and meetings remain tenaciously sedentary. Worse, planning meetings often include high sugar or empty calorie selections like chips or cookies to snack on. These are all bad snacking choices for our quest to activate deep thought processes. If you are going to put out food, try fruit and vegetables. People pick up what is offered.

Since most organizations do not openly promote standing or moving desks, or meetings that include movement, there are simple ways to work around these obstacles. Take advantage of whatever brief lunch break you have to walk around your school, or a nearby park or path. Encourage individuals to *walk and talk*, during the many micro conversations we all participate in every day to manage school and classroom operations.

Share research on the value of movement to amplify your combined creative thought processes. One popular example of this in education is the Edcamp, discussed earlier, which promotes short bursts of engaging information sharing, quick changes, and rapid movement to the next spot to learn and discuss an idea or innovation. Participants are found to be moving from one event to the next in a brisk, energized fashion.

## Block Out Blue Light

We are all surrounded by blue light, which is a light contrast that is naturally projected by the sun, but also beams out from smartphones and tablets. If you own either, you can count on being overexposed to this focus-busting byproduct of our digital engagement. As if the argument to refrain from too much digital activity is not a strong enough rationale, the harmful effects from blue light may be more evidence to convince individuals to refrain from overexposure.

Our bodies evolved to receive an adequate amount of exposure to blue light from the sun. Yet with the excessive amount of time spent on smartphones and computers, artificial sources of blue light compound this. Overexposure generates exceedingly high levels of cortisol and adrenaline. Cortisol is the body's main stress hormone, and it plays an important role in our response to danger. Adrenaline similarly flares up when the body needs to respond with an abundance of energy to counter a dangerous or exciting circumstance.

Both hormones have the effect of tapping into our primal senses in an automatic and instinctive manner. Because of the high demand placed on our body by being flooded with cortisol and adrenaline, a massive amount of energy is required. This taxing on the body does a job on us physiologically, wearing us out and causing considerable exhaustion. Worse, the symptoms of blue light flooding our eyes due to cortisol and adrenaline result in stress, anxiety and even depression.

So, what are we to do if the exposure to blue light causes disruptive symptoms that keep us from deep work and worse, adds to our anxiety? Since we are so dependent upon our devices, eliminating our digital use is unrealistic. Instead, educators looking to reduce stress and anxiety from blue light, to enhance attention and sharpness can follow several simple steps.

## Blue Light Screen Blockers

Cheap and accessible, blue light screen blockers are considered effective at significantly reducing the amount of exposure we get, from our phones, computers, and tablets. Protective screens are common for cell phones, which serve as a protective layer to prevent shattering when they are dropped. A quick online search yields the consumer plenty of options. Rather than buying a run of the mill screen protector, search for "blue light blocker" screen protectors. These are inexpensive, typically $10, or less.

The same applies for computer and tablet screens. Just be sure to know the screen dimensions to purchase the right size or cut the blue light screen protector down to size. One educator observed anecdotally that by applying this cover, he felt an immediate effect on how much his level of stress dropped and importantly, how much more soundly he slept at night. Sleep certainly is a factor and the rituals we practice at night impact our restfulness, as well as our wakefulness.

## Be Off of Digital Media Before Bed

Being on digital media may feel like an entertaining, low key pursuit for many of us who appreciate it as a part of our nighttime ritual. We feel as though we are winding down for the day and checking in becomes a common practice. Yet the blue light coming out of our devices invades our eyes and strains our senses into restlessness.

Find an alternative routine, for at least the final hour (preferably two) before trying to sleep for the night. This allows the body's natural wakefulness antidote, melatonin to settle in and keep our circadian rhythm on schedule, helping us fall asleep more naturally, and avoiding restless and wide-awake feelings of tossing and turning.

This helps the body reset and sharpens our focus in a way that capitalizes on our biological systems for fostering the methods our physiology capitalizes on for deep work. Consider selecting alternative wind-down habits, like listening to relaxing music, or reading a book under dim lighting. If you must, consider it as a last resort to watch your favorite TV program, but instead of viewing from television, use your new blue-blocked phone or tablet. Just be mindful that the alerts on your phone foster another distraction if you decide to view from a device.

## Rewire Your Brain: Practice Daily, Short-Term Gratitude Exercises

Gratitude is like the numerous small positive phrases' students can subconsciously make to gain courage, or accomplish a task, whether it be in sports, or the right mindset to focus on a test. Like this self-talk, gratitude involves consciously tapping our subconscious in constructive ways. Many self-improvement programs advocate ways to encourage our wellness through mindfulness exercises. Specifically, exercising gratitude shows benefits.

While blue light stimulates cortisol and adrenaline, gratitude, hormones, which include serotonin and dopamine, are triggered through active practices of gratitude. All individuals can increase their greater appreciation in thoughtful and feasible ways. Gratitude quite literally helps to engineer the resilience necessary for sharp focus and deep work by:

◆ Minimizing negative feelings and transforming thoughts resulting from these into optimistic ones.
◆ Adopting an outlook that focuses on the advantages in our lives.
◆ Being able to adapt to present circumstances, even in the face of challenge.
◆ Sustaining physical wellness and health by balancing the body's stasis and recalibrating hormonal irregularities that need to be reset.
◆ Inclining the individual to be solution, rather than problem oriented.
◆ Building and sustaining empathetic relationships.

## Gratitude Journals

Like the one sentence journal for students, gratitude journals help by getting us to frame our thoughts, in short passages. Documenting this way helps to embolden us to officially record our understanding of the appreciation we experience. This also allows us to refer to moments of gratitude, like replaying a happy family video, when we might need it most. Telegraph your gratitude messages for self-affirmation later.

With the remarkable benefits of practicing gratitude through simple exercises, a set of gratitude techniques for the educator can be applied on a car ride, a moment of solitude in the bathroom, or even on a quick break between meetings. This may seem trivial, but those moments literally help reset your focus, and are well worth the commitment to your wellness.

### Comparison Is the Thief of Joy. – Theodore Roosevelt

In 12-step programs, addicts are reminded to apply the logic that it is best to identify, not compare. Indeed, social media is one of the worst enemies of our human inclination to compare. We see others demonstrating the highlights of their lives, and think, *how come I can't have that*? Of course, what we do not see, are all the stumbling blocks and challenges that frustrate and challenge everyone showing off their exclusive highlight reel.

Those moments are conveniently filtered out. Comparison disrupts our gratitude as we struggle with the Fear of Missing Out (FOMO). It locks us into a have-not mentality, disregarding the opportunity that we can instead see the moments to be grateful in our lives and the gifts we have been given. A practical remedy for this is to limit our social media use and to frame perspective with guiding prompts:

### Make a Conscious Effort to See the Positive Through Guiding Questions

- ◆ What have I learned today, or this week, or month?
- ◆ Who can I count on for help?
- ◆ What made me laugh?
- ◆ What is one thing I like that comes to mind?
- ◆ What is something I'm good at?

### Consider Your Obstacles and How You Can and Have Overcome Them

No one can be happy and successful all the time, nor is it possible. In fact, without struggle and challenge, we do not progress. It is the incremental moves beyond challenge and difficulty that allow us to progress. We have all been confronted with these kinds of good stressors. Seeing them and how we moved past them or make use of them to become stronger gives us the outlook to accept and even appreciate our challenges, for how we can cleverly step around them. This characterizes the concept of productive struggle, which propels us outside of our comfort zone and into new opportunities for success.

## Breathing Exercises

An educator recalled her first year teaching when she faced a child that was difficult, sassy, and seemed to push all of her buttons. In short, this boy just got under her skin. During an incident which warranted redirection, the child asked her to *get out of my face*, with a tone that was condescending, and dismissive to her authority.

This incident occurred during the teacher's lunch duty, and others were within earshot, watching the exchange unfold. It was the closest she had ever come to reacting with a response she knew she would have regretted. Snapping back at an adolescent or with aggressive body language would have put her in a losing position, no matter what. To make matters worse, this child's parent was known for ripping teachers into shreds in defense of his son. Inexperienced and unsure of what to do, she escorted the child the short distance to the office, and removed herself from the situation, as she took a walk around the school.

During the moments that followed, she became keenly aware of her breathing. It felt rapid and uncomfortable. Clearly, her adrenaline was pumping. Remembering an article, she had once read about breathing exercises, and knowing she had to be back to teach in front of her class as classes were soon changing, she slowed her breathing down, and took deeper, timed breaths. Within a couple of minutes, she was able to effectively reset.

Not only did she have time to get back to her classroom, but she was also able to go to the office first, sit down next to this student and address him. Of course, he tested her, but she sustained her dignity and professionalism and set the stage for a follow up call with his father. Sure, as expected, this parent tested her as well, yet she justified how the situation was managed – all because of two minutes of slowing down and consciously controlling her breathing.

Schools are fast-paced places, and because of the many moments teachers experience like this, getting back to perspective fast is essential. Whether new or a seasoned teacher, this affects all of us, and accessing a technique like this is sometimes the only means available, especially since teachers are situated in a considerably autonomous space in their class, without other collegial assistance at the ready.

Teachers then must be able to apply a self-managed practice, fast and effective. We all bring with us this one resource, our breath that helps manage our reactions and instincts. This can work in a lunchroom, when encountering an aggressive parent, or during a road rage incident while running an errand. These events hit us when we least expect them to and having a familiar strategy in place that we all have access to, like breath management is vital. Let us consider the way in which we can get into this calming technique with the resourcefulness necessary, doing so rapidly and self-sustained, like our new teacher did.

Naturally, there are apps and abundant YouTube videos for quick reference, but given the common scenario of the classroom teacher, accessing this may not be viable. Pulling out your phone and stepping away during an interaction in class is not a realistic way to deal with a fast-paced moment at work. The 4–7–8 method is one quick, concealed way to apply breathing techniques to manage stress quickly and effectively. Following is a brief instruction for how to practice this exercise.

Place the tip of your tongue against the roof of your mouth, behind your two front teeth. Try to keep your tongue in this position for the duration. Within the course of a single breath, part your lips and exhale all breath with a whooshing sound through your mouth. Now shut your lips and inhale through your nose, mentally counting to four. Next, hold your breath for a silent count of seven seconds. Finally, breath out from your mouth for eight seconds with another big whoosh. Repeat, as necessary.

This works because of the beneficial exchange of incoming oxygen for outgoing carbon dioxide. In fact, this type of breathing slows your heart rate and can lower or stabilize blood pressure, all enemies of a calm, sedated mindset. It has even been described as a "natural tranquilizer for the nervous system" (Dr. Weil – Integrative Medicine, Healthy Lifestyles & Happiness, 2019). Diaphragm breathing like this are plentiful; a method like the 4–7–8 is simple and easy to remember.

## Five-Minute Phone Meditations

There are ways we can use our phones to reverse the effects caused by disruption and anxiety. Since phones are constantly by our side, harnessing the tools they offer within to help sharpen our focus is sensible. One strategy is five-minute phone meditations. Like the breathing technique described earlier, this exercise has the benefit of being quick and self-sustained. It is helpful to remove yourself from a frenzied condition as you push away distractors and disruptors. A sufficient way to achieve this is in the privacy of your car, a bathroom stall, or anywhere you can find a few minutes of privacy.

Remember, this is for just five minutes, practically short like the song *Weightless* presented earlier, and offers a quick impact. There is a narrator, taking you through a series of stationary relaxation techniques. For this reason, be sure to find one or two of these to have handy, like on an Internet search of "*5-Minute Meditation You Can Do Anywhere* (2019)." Like so many of the strategies offered throughout this text, brief meditations are easy to access, quick to reduce anxiety, free, and simply require a pair of earphones connected to your device.

Wellness has been discussed for teacher care, since educators must care for themselves before they can help children in need. This also serves as an important reminder that lifelong wellness matters and affects every part of our lives, including and especially in our professional capacity. Educators influence children, and we should be equipped to do so in positive and productive ways. In fact, getting there helps you to move to a higher level if you have set the stage in this manner. Reaching next level success will be discussed in the upcoming chapter.

## Chapter Summary

Teachers, in the trenches focused on the day to day demands and increasing challenges confronting students in great need, must learn to take care of themselves before they can help their students. A big part of this is countering challenges faced by social media. This includes the social media obstacles that distract and distort us away from a more focused, less hostile environment as we get bombarded by social media.

Social media also becomes a reality in educational leaders' day-to-day challenges in shifting the fiction spread online, as a part of our modern-day era. Use wise techniques as outlined in this text to adeptly, efficiently, and effectively counter this.

Music therapy is recognized to reduce anxiety, especially with well-chosen melodies. These are referenced and available online.

Deep work has the qualitative effect of not only helping us feel productive, but also the ability to be motivated and deeply satisfied with that work. This has the effect of reversing feelings of angst for educators.

Additional strategies to increase deep focus include reducing exposure to low cognitive-level television, scheduling time for deep work, allowing for boredom to induce creative thought, and mind-body movement.

Blue light blockers may screen us from the harmful effects of blue light that trigger stress hormones like cortisol and adrenaline, increasing unnecessary aggression and anxiety. Invest in cheap screen protectors on your devices to reduce this exposure.

Be off devices before bed, to allow the natural circadian rhythm to serve us as we allow the body to rest naturally.

Gratitude exercises literally help us rewire our brain and shift our focus to a mindset that is more constructive than destructive. Consider gratitude journals as one tool to utilize in this way.

Eliminate or reduce the moments when you are faced with comparison, because these make you think about what you do not have as opposed to what you already do and can make use of. Remember too that difficulties can be viewed as opportunities, rather than obstacles.

We all bring with us one resource that helps us control our reactions and instincts, our breath. Learning how to manage it is vital in our own wellness, especially in those unpredictable moments.

Five-minute phone meditations are quick and sustained and can be used practically almost anywhere to calm us.

# 10
# Next Level Success – Putting It All Together to Step Into Flow

Deep and focused work were discussed, because achieving high levels of success result in incredibly qualitative satisfaction. This is a tremendous remedy for anxiety and stress. Once an individual can more readily access the states that generate enhanced wellness, she becomes primed for even greater opportunities, and that is where success accelerates. It is not optimal to depend on incidental levels of high achievement that happen by accident. This is an insufficient approach, especially since we can activate higher states of performance by setting up the right conditions for it.

The objective of this guidebook has been to provide the practitioner with tools to aid students in how they achieve and grow through and beyond their trauma. Next-level success was not a focal point, since getting there had to be at the next level, after someone can center their own wellness. Certainly, there is tremendous value in higher-level achievement. Yet the priority and focus developed throughout this book was to attack the acute challenges and impact the child quickly and effectively.

DOI: 10.4324/9781003162971-10

While readers of this text are offered ways to manage difficult circumstances, there certainly is value in next-level, highly focused success. Therefore, this chapter is dedicated to the attainment of remarkable achievement, beyond the norm. Next-level success takes more time and is less urgent than the care needed to help children suffering the impact of trauma and distress. Otherwise, there would be a prescription on how to foster it and we would all be next-level superheroes.

Deep and focused work gets you to the gateway of next level success. A committed and sustained effort at managing this is what keeps a person coming back for more and reaching their ceiling. This is not pie in the sky fantasy. Authors and researchers Kotler and Wheal (2018) refer to this phenomenal level of production as "flow," and he borrows the term from an earlier researcher Mihaly Csikszentmihalyi (2008), who characterized this state as being completely absorbed in a task, while experiencing a loss in the awareness of space and time, as if to be operating from a subconscious state.

For most of us at one time or another, a flow state has happened accidentally without preparation for it, or was unexpected, because we unintentionally arranged the conditions for entering the state. Upon reflection, when individuals experience this next level mindset, they typically asserted the following occurred.

## Heightened Focus on the Work In-the-Moment

A consolidation of the process happening and one's awareness of it include the act and one's own consciousness feeling integrated together with the following identifying features:

1. An absence of self-consciousness, while totally engrossed.
2. A tremendous sense of personal control over one's circumstances, beyond normal.

3. A contortion of the consciousness of time, where it seems to disappear, or change speed (where did the time go?).
4. Self-stimulating experience – the exercise itself is intrinsically satisfying, rather than the anticipated result.

Achieving a state of flow is not easy, and that is a substantial reason it is not referenced as a tool in the three-step process for learners to grow beyond their trauma that sits at the center of this book's theme. Yet the potential dividend is profound and therefore, worth exploring. Kotler and Wheal (2018) reference extreme sports and how athletes have blown past previously unimaginable record-setting performances, because of their persistent push upward, to a flow state. These athletes shatter record after record, because of their ability to access this state.

Flow is related to deep work in that it requires a tremendous amount of energy. Therefore, anyone seeking to achieve it, whether by physical or cognitive means, should understand that the high rate of energy which flow demands results in the necessity to rest as part of the cycling process to achieve flow, and return to this state again. Thus, we cannot be in a constant state of flow without breaks. Understanding this cycling process is important to best access this level of consciousness.

Having established that achievement of a flow state requires sustained hard work, and that the gain is worth it, how do we get there? Kotler (2014) offers a path forward to accomplish this goal. He characterizes the exceptional circumstances in which a state of flow is achieved. In fact, this state is stimulated when taking unbelievable risks, or being faced with astonishing circumstances, which arouses the body and/or mind in a way that the stage is set for a vigorous response.

Fortunately, those promoting the payoff of a heightened flow state of mind and body do not propose we place ourselves in dangerous situations. Researchers and practitioners propose uncovering safer shortcuts to reach this level of peak performance. While there are many ways to achieve a state of flow, Kotler (Jim Kwik, 2018) highlights four.

1. Establishing a deep work focus helps induce a state of flow.
2. Challenge must be slightly harder than what you already know (flow sits on a border between boredom and anxiety).
3. Clear goals (not "world peace," but instead writing four pages about world peace, for example).
4. Immediate feedback must be experienced as a result of the task.

These four components work together as interconnected modalities to provoke the experience of high performance. To activate the physiological markers for stepping into these and other strategies for reaching flow, Kotler (2014) identifies that the person must first understand the basics of how flow works, and second uses this understanding to employ methods that maximize their ability to reach and sustain it, because it is also a highly individualized process.

Think about a flow state as a temporary experience, that must be managed to access the benefits derived from achieving it. Because gaining access to a flow state is so physiologically demanding and requires such tremendous energy consumption, no one truly *lives* there. Instead, people can and do *visit* there. To do so with a person's ultimate potential, it is necessary to cycle through phases, from this deep state of focus to rest.

Four stages are recommended by Kotler (2014) to avoid over-taxing the body and mind while tapping into this high level of mind-body consciousness.

### The Four Phases of Flow
a) Priming state (let it be messy but do not attach to frustration).
b) Release/relaxation (to remove the struggle).

c) Flow state (a very big high), stay focused to seize on it, you can stretch your potential to unimagined heights.

d) Recovery period – learning and memory consolidation take place; flow is expensive, a large energy consumer, and it tires you out. So, rest!

Engaging in this sequence is not only a sensible idea. Indeed, actively doing so, based on the evidence that has been presented is a worthwhile venture for those who have managed their distress and can seek out this opportunity for next level success. Following are several practical ways to provide the ideal scenario for doing so.

## Single Tasking

One of the great disservices of our fast-paced world and Western society are that we are constantly bombarded with relentless, multiple stimuli. It is no wonder that some would claim our attention spans have decreased to the level of a goldfish. These distractions and our efforts to perform multiple tasks at one time are the enemy of flow. Singular focus allows a person the ability to tap biological capacity to laser focus because we are not distracted by the other stimuli that pull us away from more qualitative vigilance and concentration.

There are many distractions that can pull us out of a highly concentrated state and hinder our ability to get there in the first place. Those distractors that are constantly giving us primal dopamine hits are what impede our ability to reach flow. Dopamine is not a bad thing. Rather, being lulled into our body's biological pleasures by external, unfocused stimuli are what pull us away from transcending states of cognition.

These alluring distractors include social media, binge TV, cell phone alerts, and more. Note that the examples provided are all digital. These are new disruptions from a historical perspective and are exponentially more profound than other distractors. Yet distractors can be different for each of us and understanding what obstructs our ability to focus is important to making flow states work for you.

## Essentialism

Single-tasking taken next level is referred to as essentialism – an outlook that inspires the individual to eliminate all unnecessary distractors. These are aspects of our lives that we may feel compelled to discard, yet often find ourselves lulled into, over and over again. We examine these principles and determine the significance of them.

One of the first distractors in many of our daily routines is our phone and, associated with it, the messaging that bombards us from the start; be it email, social media, or workstation messages. By making this accessibility constant, we have effectively laid our focus at the mercy of these low performance disruptions, almost incessantly. We have in fact, become prisoners to these attention hogs.

At its core, essentialism proposes that the person makes a choice to be extremely selective about the fundamental priorities in their life and mercilessly abandon everything else. This may sound like a daunting, implausible goal. Yet absent the pursuit to become a monk in a sheltered monastery, we should decide to pragmatically become essential only some of the time, for some priorities.

Almost everyone has fallen victim to this daily barrage of distractions and like the goldfish, it is easy to see why we get pulled into other directions, away from truly remarkable and deeply sustained work. So, what are we to do? Making a choice to schedule email responses, where possible, especially for later in the day is one practical solution.

Our brains are wired for a heightened level of focus and energy earlier in our wake cycle, in the morning. This is when our prefrontal cortex, or creative brain processing center is most active. Therefore, this time is naturally when our brains are most calibrated to work productively and enter a state of flow. Where possible, preserve this time for that creativity and avoid digital distractions.

This is where the dilemma often enters. We feel responsible, even guilty if we are not checking in on a regular basis. That is our most deliberate mistake. One educational leader put it this way: *there are now and later decisions.* Now decisions are when there is smoke coming out of the vent, or a child is on the floor, having a seizure. That is a "now" decision. Throw deep work and flow out the window. Act now. These now decisions are small in proportion and you will know when they occur and need to act.

Later decisions are almost everything else. They are questions that can be followed up on, perhaps within hours, days, or weeks. In fact, a simple way to manage later decisions is to ground your response to expectant others in the rationale that you will respond in a timely fashion, typically one school or business day. Yet make clear that the inquiry or request is important for you to address, and so you want to make an informed decision, one that is not a rushed, automated judgement. People most often understand and appreciate the patience in responding, when presented in this manner. Subsequently, you have time to remain undistracted.

Leveraging this vast majority of responses for later in the day also frequently nets the common refrain, *never mind, I figured it out* reaction, from others. This is in fact a bonus for both you and the other person because you are not micromanaging, and they are learning skills of problem solving and independence in your immediate absence. This has the added effect of people coming to the realization that while you will be responsive, a prompt, if not immediate reaction is reasonable, and liberates them to realize that they often can figure it out on their own.

Being temporarily, and strategically, unreachable almost never causes a concern and if someone truly needs to get a hold of you, they can typically find you. It is not rude; in fact, this approach can be delivered as a more systematic way to address issues and needs. One principal provided this rationale in his notice to families, and it has stood the test of time, political structural changes and more, as a sustainable and justified approach. This resource is available in Appendix F for educational leaders and teachers alike to adopt and adapt, giving hesitation an allowance in our thoughtful response time.

Finding ways to reduce and possibly eliminate persistent fragmentation of our attention that creates such a dysfunctional part of our everyday lives is established as a universal challenge. Newport (2019) reminds us with science and practical advice about all this interference, and how to counter it. Consider all the tabs open on a computer, analogous to your brain with that many tabs open. It is no wonder we are so flustered as we seek to sort and navigate through all those tabs.

Those mind tabs offer a comparison to demonstrate the need to eliminate digital and other distractors. These and other suggestions to follow are what truly motivates the individual beyond those obstacles and into enhanced states of flow, setting the stage for high level work performance and with it, tremendous satisfaction, a big payoff for our own well-being.

This has the dual effect of netting high performance and connecting the successful work to elevated degrees of deep personal satisfaction. A qualitative level of fulfillment returns us to our chief goal of helping all individuals to foster improved wellness, beyond their circumstances of distress. Striking a balance is not only an ideal upper limit, it relates closely to sustained growth and long term wellness. That is why music was discussed and will be reviewed again to achieve accelerated levels of productivity and satisfaction.

## Music

Music, and more specifically the incorporation of evidence-based anxiety reducing binaural beat sounds to tune the brain, was discussed in the main section of this text on trauma. Music and melody have been presented with the primary objective of reducing the effects of stress, anxiety, and trauma. Established is well-founded evidence that listening to music can help to achieve calmness and lowered states of anxiety.

What is beneficial about music, and the scientific backed effects of listening to it, is that it can also help us to achieve a higher state of mind. Like all other components of this section, this can only be achieved once the impacts of trauma and distress caused by it are managed. Then and only then, can we activate a higher state, navigating our mindset slightly in a different direction, one that taps into our prefrontal cortex. This is achieved by accessing the right brain waves and striking the correct balance between them.

*Alpha and Theta brain waves*: To know the type of music and melody that most affects each state of mind, it is useful to understand the two types of brain waves we can experience through binaural beats to achieve a disproportionately higher productive capacity. The binaural concept happens when you are exposed to two tones, one at differing levels in each ear.

These two tones are purposely varied in frequency, so your brain processes a beat at the difference of the frequencies, called a binaural beat. Prefrontal stimulation is switched on when alpha and theta wave signals are sent into each ear to cause this effect. What do each of these have the effect of doing to our mind and body and how does it help to trigger flow-like capacity?

Theta waves have the effect of inducing a strong internal focus such as meditation, mindfulness, and spiritual awareness. When optimized, they promote adaptive, complex behaviors such as learning and memory at higher states of consciousness. *Caution*: because a level of theta that is too high or out of balance can, in fact, increase anxiety, be mindful of this intricate balance. Therefore, it is vital to include alpha waves in the mix, and at the right frequency.

Alpha waves, interacting with theta waves through binaural beats integration at the correct binaural decibel level, present a pattern of sound that helps us to achieve a flow state. Your brain produces alpha waves when you are not focusing too hard on anything specifically. There is a strong sense of calm and relaxation produced by alpha wave stimulation. Following is a description of how the two work so well together and why this balance helps us to achieve a desired flow state.

The alpha-theta interaction at a sound level of 8 Hz places us in a state that is on the border between the conscious and the subconscious mind. When a person experiences this level of intense creativity, they experience a theta burst where engagement in deep telegraphing within this higher state occurs. This is where performance can be considerably heightened. Here, many people describe "being in the zone" where their work feels effortless, timeless, and deeply rewarding.

Alpha-theta regulation positions a person's mindset between their conscious and subconscious mind. The closest natural analogy to this is when we are on the verge of wakefulness, between sleep and consciousness. Unknowingly, some of our greatest thoughts can thrive in this state. Competitive athletes seek out this state of consciousness; a sweet spot where robust creativity and optimal performance takes place. This is the mindset where people have the power to combine accelerated decisions and creative insight.

Alpha-theta regulation, like all competing brain wave states, requires that theta waves are dominant over the alpha waves, which can be considered a high theta, low alpha medium. With the knowledge of alpha-theta binaural integration and the ability to exceed our normal state of productivity and creativity, there are many ways to engage melody, sounds and music. This allows us to settle into a calm enough state yet one that does not make us overly relaxed, from a lighter dose of theta wave effects.

At the same time, we heighten the focus and concentration at a greater rate. This rate is levelled just enough to strike that extreme creativity balance, innovative thought and mindfulness brought on by alpha brain waves. A simple search online for high theta, low alpha binaural music will yield many options, for the reader to engage in right away, and when they desire to establish parameters to return to establishing the conditions for next-level success in the future.

The most optimal effect is caused by listening in an undisturbed location, with earbuds or headphones on, since you want the alternate sounds entering from each ear via opposing sides of the brain. Be aware that underlying medical conditions, such as a pacemaker or other comorbid conditions should mean the individual proceeds with extreme caution when engaging in the listening of binaural beats or other sound remedies. Always consult a physician if you have medical concerns.

## Coffeehouse Chatter

Have you ever sat in a coffeehouse with a good book, or your laptop, and completely immersed yourself in the ambience, while productively working? This experience shelters you in the experiences of deep work and a flow state. Since a flow state is so desirable, many can relate to this, and it is not difficult to seek out, coffeehouse chatter is a proposed strategy to employ.

The arrangements for structuring time and place go beyond standard deep work tactics. Realistically, how many of our students and teachers can just excuse themselves from their role in school to cross the street to the closest coffee shop? There are other ways to mirror this experience.

There is evidence which demonstrates that a balanced delivery of ambient sound contributes to enriching levels of cognition (University of Alberta, 2019). In other words, achieving slight distraction helps you to be more creative. Therefore, those eureka moments happen, when we are conducting seemingly monotonous tasks like taking out the garbage, standing in the shower, or working in a garden. It is easy, slightly distracting work that lulls us into mind wondering. How does this work?

If not focused so much on the complexity of a task, we generate thoughts and ideas. In the coffee shop, the sounds of chatter and clatter distract us away from other higher intensity distractions that veer our minds away from the very creative work we seek. This propels us toward much higher focused, flow states. Where can you find the tools to do this, without heading out to your garden, or the local coffeehouse?

Go online and search on a web browser for "coffeehouse sounds." You will gain more from using your computer with headphones, or your cell phone, with earbuds, by obstructing other distracting noises, like sound alerts. Use background noise to present a "distracted focus," the ideal sound level of ambiguous chatter and clatter to target prefrontal cortex activity and work. Doing so allows you to enter states like or mirroring flow to produce intensely focused work.

One of the reasons flow state and research about it is so intriguing is that when you can execute it, you get disproportionate increases in innovative production. The creation of productivity skyrockets and this creates a very blissful feeling of success and productivity that high achievers experience. This level of disproportionate success is what separate high achievers from the rest. This provides a convincing rationale for why achieving this state is so appealing.

The research continues, given the complexities of our mind but the evidence is clear. Achieving a flow state when our wellness is intact causes us to outperform, to be the best version of ourselves, and in ways that surprise and inspire us. The results are long term achievement and success; well worth the sacrifices made (avoiding social media, being unavailable, etc.).

The strategies offered in this chapter are not end-alls. Rather, they are highlights of the many that can serve as a guide to elevate us into a flow state. This information was condensed for the purpose of presenting the benefits and basics for application. A quick online search for flow state will present a wealth of additional information, as related to this next level success.

This book has presented a resource to impact students' recovery from trauma, anxiety and stress, for teachers, those in the trenches who spend the most time with them. There is no silver bullet, no prescription to solve the many, varied, and complex ills resulting from the negative consequences of trauma. Additionally, this book does not suggest a clinical perspective, for those who treat the most intense and identified of our traumatized learners, often when it is too late.

Rather, this guide was composed to offer practical, in class, efficient, and impactful short-term solutions that can translate into long term success. This will not solve every child's challenges, all the time. Rather, the solutions offered within the text present options to help many kids, much of the time. These solutions are a combined approach, based on research, and years of anecdotal evidence from practitioners, showing time tested practices that can be adapted to help children recover from the effects of trauma.

Consider options like the three-step process contained in this text. Remember that not all tactics should be used all the time, nor is this practical. Rather, apply varying components, examine the results, and adapt to each individual child. Develop child-specific best practices, rather than universal applications. Remember that building rapport and developing comfort for students begins our journey.

Amassing data, analyzing, and tracking this for each child to monitor and adjust to support the child can come from data sources that are not normally thought of as conventional options, yet also come naturally as a part of teachers' instruction. This economizes the approach to collect and use data to inform about students learning and challenges.

Continue the cycle by seizing on student achievements, no matter how small and celebrate their small wins. Build momentum as a catalyst for both their progress and recovery, and their ability to learn from this skill and generalize to their own lifelong skill to manage their recovery. Remember that building rapport through fun and engaging methods, amassing natural sets of data, and celebrating small wins is a rough though not exact map for the directions we follow to support children.

This is and must always remain cyclical, with our prepared-ness to return to other parts of this three-part cycle, when it best suits the child. Allowing for both a pliability in this process and a general roadmap promotes the likelihood that more students will be better off if applying these techniques. Not all students, but many will respond well, and that is progress; that is improvement.

Remember too that professionals in classrooms helping children need to take care of themselves. Absent their own check system, they will not be able to effectively utilize, nor model these practices for their own learners. If achieved, educators and students alike can advance to levels beyond their dreams.

Adopting practices to superimpose upon an individual's conditions, the opportunity to disproportionately outperform exists, through a concept known as flow. Be prepared for this next-level success, if and when the opportunity occurs, because we all win, when students and the adults working with them are given the opportunity to flourish. That alone is worth the time to tinker with this three-step process.

## Chapter Summary

By following the three-step sequence offered in this guide, users may have found they were able to help children, and possibly themselves, with long-term wellness and recovery from trauma. If this or other resources have helped an individual, there is more; and it is exciting, promising productivity and deep satisfaction. Flow state is a concept that was presented through strong recent research to indicate that individuals could use the tools of essentialism and ambience to enhance their surroundings. In so doing, they may succeed at achieving accelerated rates of focus and flow. This results in a disproportionately beneficial yield of results. Consider the resources suggested in this text, and appendixes to try to achieve this state, and outperform at next-level success.

# Appendix A: Letter on Aerodynamic Chairs

Dear Manager,

Our school has embarked on a journey to help children succeed despite their limitations. We are working to support children who have faced trauma and distress that has caused them to be fearful and distracted from being their best self at school. You can help. With your small donation of 2–3 aerodynamic office chairs, we can include these in our research based "mindfulness room" which fosters a comfort zone for them to work out their challenges. As those helping these children in need, we know that giving them a safe place to go to and express themselves without risk is an effective technique in aiding them in their recovery from challenges. Please be part of our solution. Let us know if you have any questions, or if you would like us to promote your store because of your kind gift. Every child who enjoys the comfort of your chairs will know that you were part of their road to recovery from trauma.

Sincerely,

The Teachers and Children of _____school

# Appendix B: Sample Facilitator's Guide

## Respect

**Date:** As necessary

**Prerequisites:** None

<u>Goal</u>: Student will examine reasons that someone exhibits disrespectful behavior explain actions, defend answers to the questions provided, and present ways to minimize disrespectful interactions in the future.

<u>Vocabulary Focus</u>: respect, disrespect, self-respect, esteem, deference, character traits.

## Resources:

- ♦ Vocabulary sheet.
- ♦ Respect worksheets.
- ♦ Character Traits reference sheet.

<u>Prompt</u>: Describe the situation for which you have been assigned a Restorative Justice. *Complete Do Now Sheet.*

## Intervention Steps:

1. Collect and review Prompt response.
2. Discuss vocabulary for this activity.
3. Determine specific Respect worksheets to use.
4. Have student complete specific Respect worksheets.
5. Discuss answers to Respect worksheets with students. Focus on reasons for disrespectful behavior.

  a. Lack of self-respect
  b. Inability to moderate behavior
    i. Dislike of character traits in individual
    ii. Feeling of "unfairness"
    iii. Failure to recognize authority figure.
 **6.** Have student defend answers and explain ways to minimize future occurrences.

**Follow-up Prompt**: How can you keep a similar situation from happening in the future? *Complete Closure Sheet*.
 Put this intervention into ACTION!

## Writing Prompt

Name: _____ Date: _____
 Prompt: Describe the situation for which you have been assigned a restorative justice intervention.

_____

_____

_____

_____

_____

_____

_____

_____

_____

_____

 Follow-up Prompt: How can you keep this or a similar situation from happening again? What specific steps can you take to avoid another situation like this?

_____

_____

_____

_____

_____

_____

_____

_____

_____

_____

_____

## Respect Vocabulary

Specific Vocabulary for Respect Worksheets

**Esteem: (V)** To have a high opinion of.

**Deference: (N)** Submission to the desires, opinions, or judgments of another.

**Respect: (N)** A positive feeling of esteem or deference for a person or other entity.

**Disrespect: (N)** Lack of respect; rudeness.

**Self-respect: (N)** The proper regard for oneself and one's worth as a person.

**Character traits: (N)** A characteristic or quality that makes a person or animal different from others.

## *Activity 1*

Name:_____ Date: _____

It's about **RESPECT**

**Respect** (N): a positive feeling of esteem or deference for a person or other entity.

1. Three people in this school that I respect are:

   a. _____

   I respect this person because:

   _____

   _____

   _____

   _____

   _____

   _____

   b. _____

   I respect this person because:

   _____

   _____

   _____

   _____

   _____

   _____

   c. _____

   I respect this person because:

   _____

   _____

   _____

   _____

   _____

   _____

2. Three people outside of school I respect are:

a. _____

I respect this person because:

_____

_____

_____

_____

_____

b. _____

I respect this person because:

_____

_____

_____

_____

_____

c. _____

I respect this person because:

_____

_____

_____

_____

_____

3. Look at the list of character traits, pick **three** of the traits that you **respect the most**.

a. _____

b. _____

c. _____

Look at the list of character traits, pick **three** of the traits that you **like the least**.

a. _____

b. _____

c. _____

4.  Who was the person that you were disrespectful to and why?

    _____

    _____

    _____

    _____

## *Activity 2*

Name: _____ Date: _____

How can you use I'm More Than Just That/Behind the Curtain to be respectful to others?

a. Look for the best in others:

_____

_____

_____

b. Treat others the way you want to be treated:

_____

_____

_____

c. Choose positive influences:

_____

_____

_____

d. Speak works of kindness:

_____

_____

_____

e. Forgive yourself and others:

_____

_____

_____

## *Activity 3*

Name: _____ Date: _____

### Self-Respect

1. Look at the Character Trait list. List three trait that you possess that you think make you worthy of other people's respect.

   a. _____

   b. _____

   c. _____

2. Look at the Character Trait list. List three trait that you possess that you think are not worthy of other people's respect.

   a. _____

   b. _____

   c. _____

3. Let's focus on the traits that are not worthy of respect. What can you do to work on these to minimize their effect on your life?

   _____

   _____

   _____

## *Activity 4*

Name:_____ Date: _____

Directions:

1.  Read each of the following quotes.
2.  After each quote summarize what the quote is saying by putting it in your own words.
3.  Write which quote is your favorite and why?

"I speak to everyone in the same way, whether he is the garbage man or the president of the university."

Albert Einstein
In your own words:

_____

_____

_____

_____

_____

"Respect yourself and others will respect you."
Confucius
In your own words:

_____

_____

_____

_____

_____

"When people do not respect us we are sharply offended; yet deep down in his private heart no man much respects himself."
Mark Twain

In your own words:

_____

_____

_____

_____

_____

**"This is how you start to get respect, by offering something that you have."**
Mitch Albom
In your own words:

_____

_____

_____

_____

_____

**"Respect your efforts, respect yourself. Self-respect leads to self-discipline. When you have both firmly under your belt, that's real power."**
Clint Eastwood
In your own words:

_____

_____

_____

_____

_____

**"If you want to be respected by others the great thing is to respect yourself. Only by that, only by self-respect will you compel others to respect you."**
Fyodor Dostoyevsky
In your own words:

_____

_____

_____

_____

_____

**"Football is like life, it requires perseverance, hard work, sacrifice, dedication, respect for authority."**
Vince Lombardi
In your own words:

_____

_____

_____

_____

_____

**"If you want to be respected, you must respect yourself."**
Anonymous
In your own words:

_____

_____

_____

_____

_____

Which quote is your favorite and why?

_____

_____

_____

_____

_____

## Closure activity

Name: _____ Date: _____

### Put it into *ACTION!*

Give at least three examples of how you can show respect in the following areas/situations:

1. In the classroom:
2. In the hallways:
3. In the cafeteria:
4. On the bus:
5. During school events or assemblies:

# Appendix C: Two-Minute Intervention Worksheet

## Discussion Starters Can Be a New Discussion Point, or Continuation of What Was Previously Discussed.

Example: I noticed you wore that Lebron jersey yesterday . . .
Continuation example: Are you watching the game with Lebron playing tonight?

| Monday | Tuesday | Wednesday | Thursday | Friday |
|---|---|---|---|---|
| 2 minute discussion starter: | 2 minute discussion starter: | 2 minute discussion starter: | 2 minute discussion starter: | 2 minute discussion starter: |
| Monday | Tuesday | Wednesday | Thursday | Friday |
| 2 minute discussion starter: | 2 minute discussion starter: | 2 minute discussion starter: | 2 minute discussion starter: | 2 minute discussion starter: |

# Appendix D: The One-Sentence Intervention

Target student: _____

 List 2–3 items noticed about the target student. These are objective acknowledgements about a child's identify. They are not weighted with opinion, but a recognition that this is part of who they are, and that it has value.

 Some examples to acknowledge something specific about the child:

> *I noticed that you listen to hip hop music.*
> *I see that you have a lot of items that are purple in color.*
> *I heard that you wear a jersey of your favorite player (name player)*
>  *every time he/she plays.*

_____. I noticed . . .
_____. I see that . . .
_____. I heard that . . .

- - - - - - - - - - - - - - - - - - - - - - - - - - - - - - - -

 Note some positive changes you are starting to see in the child:

 Some examples to indicate a positive include:

> *I noticed that when you listen to music, you are more focused and*
>  *work well.*
> *I heard that you babysit your little sister so your mom can go out*
>  *once a week.*

 Indicated 2–3 positive factors you can think of that I can notice: I noticed . . . _____.
I noticed . . .

_____. I heard . . .

_____. I saw . . .

Observe behavior after 2–3 weeks of neutral and positive statements: _____

_____

# Appendix E: For Being Strategically "Unreachable"

## School Contact Procedures

The school administration believes in the importance of the link between school and home. This link provides the foundation for a successful learning experience for our students. We value regular communication between parents and those charged with educating your children. It is in the best interest of your child if, when there is a matter that you wish to address, you do so as follows:

♦ Contact the staff member closest to the issue that you would like to address. More often than not, there is a resolution with this first contact.
♦ Next, if necessary, contact the grade-level administrator.
♦ **6th Grade** . . . – – – -
♦ **7th Grade** . . . – – – -

# Bibliography

*5-Minute Meditation You Can Do Anywhere*. (2019, September 4). [Video file]. Retrieved from www.youtube.com/watch?v=inpok4MKVLM

Adams, J. M. (2017, February 16). *For teachers, it's not just what you say, it's how you say it*. Retrieved November 7, 2020, from https://edsource.org/2017/for-teachers-its-not-just-what-you-say-its-how-you-say-it/574363

Ahead in the Game. (2012, February 28). *How you say it, is proven more important than what you say . . . | aheadinthegame.ca*. Retrieved December 29, 2020, from www.aheadinthegame.ca/2012/02/how-you-say-it-is-proven-more-important-than-what-is-said/

Amabile, T., & Kramer, S. (2011). *The progress principle: Using small wins to ignite joy, engagement, and creativity at work* (1st ed.). New York, NY: Harvard Business Review Press.

American Federation of Teachers. (2020, October 22). *Educators say COVID-19 has greatly exacerbated the grief support crisis in schools, according to new survey*. Retrieved November 17, 2020, from www.aft.org/press-release/educators-say-covid-19-has-greatly-exacerbated-grief-support-crisis-schools

Ballard, E. S. (1974). *Three letters from teddy*. Retrieved July 22, 2020, from www.catholiceducation.org/en/faith-and-character/faith-and-character/three-letters-from-teddy.html

Benson, K. (2017, October 4). *The magic relationship ratio, according to science*. Retrieved October 19, 2020, from www.gottman.com/blog/the-magic-relationship-ratio-according-science/

Berwick, C. (2019, October 25). *What does the research say about testing?* Retrieved November 2, 2020, from www.edutopia.org/article/what-does-research-say-about-testing

Brame, C., & Biel, R. (2015). *Test-enhanced learning: Using retrieval practice to help students learn*. Retrieved October 15, 2020, from https://cft.vanderbilt.edu/guides-sub-pages/test-enhanced-learning-using-retrieval-practice-to-help-students-learn/

Carpenter, J. P., & Linton, J. N. (2018). Educators' perspectives on the impact of edcamp unconference professional learning. *Teaching and Teacher Education, 73*, 56–69. doi:10.1016/j.tate.2018.03.014

Center for Disease Control and Prevention. (n.d.). *Adverse childhood experiences (ACEs)*. Retrieved January 9, 2021, from www.cdc.gov/violenceprevention/aces/index.html

Csikszentmihalyi, M. (2008). *Flow: The psychology of optimal experience* (1st ed.). New York, NY: Harper Perennial Modern Classics.

Curtin, M. (n.d.). *Neuroscience says listening to this song reduces anxiety by up to 65 percent*. Retrieved June 19, 2020, from www.inc.com/melanie-curtin/neuroscience-says-listening-to-this-one-song-reduces-anxiety-by-up-to-65-percent.html

Dr. Weil – Integrative Medicine, Healthy Lifestyles & Happiness. (2019, January 7). *Three breathing exercises and techniques*. Retrieved January 5, 2021, from www.drweil.com/health-wellness/body-mind-spirit/stress-anxiety/breathing-three-exercises/

Dunlosky, J., Rawson, K. A., Marsh, E. J., Nathan, M. J., & Willingham, D. T. (2013, January 14). *Improving students' learning with effective learning techniques: Promising directions from cognitive and educational psychology*. Retrieved December 17, 2020, from https://pubmed.ncbi.nlm.nih.gov/26173288/

Dweck, C. S. (2006). *Mindset: The new psychology of success*. New York, NY: Random House.

Eagleson, C., Hayes, S., Matthews, A., Perman, G., & Hirsch, H. R. (2016, March). *The power of positive thinking: pathological worry is reduced by thought replacement in generalized anxiety disorder*. Science Direct. Retrieved from https://www.sciencedirect.com/science/article/pii/S0005796715300814?via%3Dihub

Educational Data Systems. (2018, March 1). *How assessment improves learning*. Retrieved November 3, 2020, from https://eddata.com/2018/03/assessment-improves-learning/

Eilers, E. (n.d.). *What out-of-school suspensions really cost students – and what educators can do about it*. Retrieved October 8, 2020, from www.crisisprevention.com/Blog/What-Out-of-School-Suspensions-Really-Cost

Epston, D. (2013, October 6). *An emergency response to 'going off your face' at school.* Retrieved January 10, 2021, from www.narrativeapproaches.com/2968-2/

Gambini, B. (2018, September 26). *Your Facebook friends don't mean it, but they're likely hurting you daily.* Retrieved October 22, 2020, from www.buffalo.edu/news/releases/2018/09/034.html

Garcia, E., & Weiss, E. (2020, September 10). *COVID-19 and student performance, equity, and U.S. education policy: Lessons from pre-pandemic research to inform relief, recovery, and rebuilding.* Retrieved November 19, 2020, from www.epi.org/publication/the-consequences-of-the-covid-19-pandemic-for-education-performance-and-equity-in-the-united-states-what-can-we-learn-from-pre-pandemic-research-to-inform-relief-recovery-and-rebuilding/

Gaskell, M. S. (2020). *Microstrategy magic* (Illustrated ed.). New York, NY: Rowman & Littlefield.

Gooblar, D. (2018, October 10). *When you communicate with students, tone matters.* Retrieved January 9, 2021, from https://community.chronicle.com/news/2115-when-you-communicate-with-students-tone-matters

Hardy, D. (2012). *The compound effect* (CSM ed.). New York, NY: Vanguard Press.

*How to: Use the Power of Personal Connection to Motivate Students: 4 Strategies.* (n.d.). Intervention Central. Retrieved January 7, 2021, from https://www.interventioncentral.org/blog/behavior/how-use-power-personal-connection-motivate-students-4-strategies

Ismail, S., Malone, M. S., Geest, V. Y., & Diamandis, P. H. (2014). *Exponential organizations: Why new organizations are ten times better, faster, and cheaper than yours (and what to do about it).* New York, NY: Diversion Books.

Jim Kwik. (2018, October 29). *Kwik brain episode 20: Hacking flow for faster learning with Steven Kotler* [Video]. YouTube. Retrieved from https://www.youtube.com/watch?v=wznxlxPf0YQ

Kahoot. (2021, January 15). *How do I get reports with results of my challenges?* Retrieved from https://support.kahoot.com/hc/en-us/

articles/115016115248-How-do-I-get-reports-with-results-of-my-challenges

Koch, A. B. (2017, February 14). *Sounds of education: Teacher role and use of voice in interactions with young children.* Retrieved September 18, 2020, from https://link.springer.com/article/10.1007/s13158-017-0184-6?error=cookies_not_supported&code=aee85fcf-3184-436b-b654-36937646215f

Kotler, S. (2014). *The rise of superman: Decoding the science of ultimate human performance* (1st ed.). New York, NY: New Harvest.

Kotler, S., & Wheal, J. (2018). *Stealing fire: How Silicon Valley, the navy seals, and maverick scientists are revolutionizing the way we live and work* (Reprint ed.). New York, NY: Dey Street Books.

Kross, E., Bruehlman-Senecal, E., Park, J., Burson, A., Dougherty, A., Shablack, H., . . . Ayduk, O. (2014). Self-talk as a regulatory mechanism: How you do it matters. *Journal of Personality and Social Psychology, 106*(2), 304–324. doi:10.1037/a0035173

Lahey, J. (2014, January 21). *Students should be tested more, not less.* Retrieved June 16, 2020, from www.theatlantic.com/education/archive/2014/01/students-should-be-tested-more-not-less/283195/

*Mail Merge from Excel to Microsoft Word.* (2020, June 1). [Video file]. Retrieved from www.youtube.com/watch?v=mFqCvTOpOL0

McKibben, S. (2014, July). *The two-minute relationship builder.* ASCD Education Update. http://www.ascd.org/publications/newsletters/education_update/jul14/vol56/num07/The_Two-Minute_Relationship_Builder.aspx

McMinn, D. (2017, July 26). *Make your bed every morning – generate "success momentum".* Retrieved August 18, 2020, from https://donmcminn.com/2017/07/make-bed-every-morning-generate-success-momentum/?doing_wp_cron=1606704039.4595310688018798828125

Miller, G. M. (2018, November 29). *Post-traumatic growth & resiliency factors for children and adolescents.* Retrieved September 7, 2020, from https://starr.org/post-traumatic-growth-resiliency-factors-for-children-and-adolescents/

Minahan, J. (2019, October). *Trauma-informed teaching strategies – educational leadership.* Educational Leadership. http://www.ascd.

org/publications/educational_leadership/oct19/vol77/num02/
Trauma-Informed_Teaching_Strategies.asp

Nearpod. (n.d.). *Security check*. Retrieved January 6, 2021, from https://
nearpod.zendesk.com/hc/en-us/articles/203701949-How-to-access-
post-session-student-responses-with-Nearpod-reports

Newman, S. (2015, April 8). *The power of the one-sentence journal*.
Retrieved September 19, 2020, from https://psychcentral.com/
blog/the-power-of-the-one-sentence-journal#1

Newport, C. (2019). *Digital minimalism: Choosing a focused life in a
noisy world*. New York, NY: Portfolio.

Oaklander, M. (2020, August 5). *3 ways creativity can help mental
health, from the musician jewel*. Retrieved December 15,
2020, from https://time.com/5875144/jewel-mental-health-
creativity/

Olson, J. (2013). *The slight edge* (Anniversary ed.). Austin, TX: Success
Books.

Padlet. (2021, January 4). *Padlet: You are beautiful*. Retrieved from
https://padlet.com/

Patel, N., Smith, R., Fitzsimmons, K., Kara, M. G., & Detmer, E. (2012).
Utilizing goal setting strategies at the middle level: Helping
students self-regulate behavior. *Networks: An Online Journal for
Teacher Research, 14*(2), 1–9. doi:10.4148/2470-6353.1072

Pathway 2 Success. (n.d.). *101 positive affirmations for kids*. Retrieved
December 8, 2020, from www.thepathway2success.
com/101-positive-affirmations-for-kids/

Paul, A. M., & Paul, A. M. (2015, August 1). *Researchers find that
frequent tests can boost learning*. Retrieved November 18, 2020,
from www.scientificamerican.com/article/researchers-find-
that-frequent-tests-can-boost-learning/

Peardeck. (n.d.). *Can I export student responses?* Retrieved January 5,
2021, from https://help.peardeck.com/can-i-export-student-
responses#example

Reading Workshop. (n.d.). *Guided reading and reading workshop*.
Retrieved February 25, 2021, from http://guidedreadingsbs.
weebly.com/reading-workshop.html

Rotter, J. B. (1954). *Social learning and clinical psychology*. New York:
Prentice-Hall.

*"Save as Doc" Google Sheets Add on (How to use)*. (2020, May 22). [Video file]. Retrieved from www.youtube.com/watch?v=_DpjPrpo_cI

*Self-Select Breakout Rooms in Zoom | Allow Participants to Choose Breakout Room*. (2020, September 28). [Video file]. Retrieved from www.youtube.com/watch?v=mmZ0Yo0zWBk

Sherrington, T. (2017, March 26). *The bell-curve cage: Something must break*. Retrieved June 11, 2020, from https://teacherhead.com/2017/03/26/the-bell-curve-cage-something-must-break/

Shpancer, N. (2020, December 9). *A science-based technique for coping with stress, how you speak to yourself matters*. Retrieved December 28, 2020, from www.psychologytoday.com/us/blog/insight-therapy/202012/science-based-technique-coping-stress

Smith, R. (2019, June 18). *How to make your small wins work for you*. Retrieved September 20, 2020, from https://ideas.ted.com/how-to-make-your-small-wins-work-for-you/

Speech Notes. (n.d.). *Speech to text online notepad, free*. Retrieved December 19, 2020, from https://speechnotes.co/

TEDx Chilliwack. (2018, May 4). *To achieve success, start detecting your small wins | Mehrnaz Bassiri | TEDxChilliwack* [Video]. YouTube. Retrieved from https://www.youtube.com/watch?v=qxGapZbbI38

University of Alberta. (2019, October 21). *Make some noise: How background noise affects brain activity: Scientists take neuroscience outside the lab, investigating how different sorts of background noise affect our focus*. Retrieved November 2, 2020, from www.sciencedaily.com/releases/2019/10/191021093957.htm

University of Michigan. (2018, September 13). *Suspending young students risks future success in school*. Retrieved December 22, 2020, from www.sciencedaily.com/releases/2018/09/180913134540.htm

University of Wisconsin – Madison Psychology Department. (n.d.). *Rosenthal's work on expectancy effects*. Retrieved October 23, 2020, from http://psych.wisc.edu/braun/281/Intelligence/LabellingEffects.htm

VanDeBrake, J. (2018, September 27). *The science of storytelling: Why we love stories – the startup*. Retrieved August 10, 2020, from https://medium.com/swlh/the-science-of-storytelling-why-we-love-stories-fceb3464d4c3

Vollmer, J. (2011, November 8). *The blueberry story: The teacher gives the businessman a lesson.* Retrieved July 17, 2020, from https://newsroom.unl.edu/announce/csmce/755/3329

Werner, E. E., & Smith, R. S. (2001). *Journeys from childhood to midlife: Risk, resilience, and recovery* (1st ed.). Ithaca, NY: Cornell University Press.

*What is Nearpod?.* (2020, August 6). [Video file]. Retrieved from www.youtube.com/watch?v=cYVHSAqEeMM